W9-CTK-471

DATE DUE


```
              $19.95
  942.05    Shakespeare's
  Sha         England
```

01597

SHAKESPEARE'S ENGLAND

Library Edition published 1989
Published by Marshall Cavendish Corporation
147 West Merrick Road
Freeport, Long Island
N.Y. 11520

Typeset by Jamesway Graphics
Hanson Close Middleton Manchester M24 2HD
Printed in the USA by Worzalla Publishing
Company, Wisconsin

All rights reserved. No part of this book may be
reproduced or utilized in any form or by any
means electronic or mechanical including
photocopying, recording, or by an information
storage and retrieval system, and without
permission from the copyright holder.

© Marshall Cavendish Limited
MCMLXXXVIII, MCMLXXXIX

LIBRARY OF CONGRESS
Library of Congress Cataloging-in-Publication
Data

Shakespeare's England.
    p. cm. — (Exploring the past: 6)
    Bibliography: p.
    Includes index.
    Summary: Describes the lives and times of
Henry VIII, Elizabeth I, and William
Shakespeare.
    ISBN 0–86307–999–7: $19.95.
    ISBN 0–86307–993–8 (set): $119.95
    1. Great Britain — History — Tudors.
1485-1603 — Biography — Juvenile literature.
2. Henry VIII. King of England, 1491-1547 —
Juvenile literature. 3. Elizabeth I, Queen of
England, 1533-1603 — Juvenile literature.4.
Shakespeare, William, 1564-1616 — Biography
— Juvenile literature. 5. Shakespeare, William,
1564-1616 — Contemporary England —
Juvenile literature. 6. Great Britain — Kings
and rulers — Biography — Juvenile literature.
7. Dramatists, English — Early modern,
1500-1700 — Biography — Juvenile literature.
[1. Great Britain — History — Tudors,
1485-1603. 2. Henry VIII, King of England,
1491-1547. 3. Elizabeth I, Queen of England,
1533-1603. 4. Kings, queens, rulers, etc. 5.
Shakespeare, William, 1564-1616. 6. Authors,
English.] I. Marshall Cavendish Corporation. II.
Series.
DA317.S46 1989   88–21646
942.05—dc19   CIP
                                                AC

ISBN 0–86307–993–8 (set)
ISBN 0–86307–999–7 (vol)

Shakespeare's England is number six in the
Exploring the Past series.

Credits: Front cover: Stephen Biesty;
page 1: Graham Humphries

SHAKESPEARE'S
ENGLAND

Henry VIII

Elizabeth I

William Shakespeare

Marshall Cavendish

NEW YORK · TORONTO · LONDON · SYDNEY

015970

CASTILLERO MIDDLE SCHOOL
6384 LEYLAND PARK DRIVE
SAN JOSE, CA 95120

STAFF LIST

Series Editor
Sue Lyon

Assistant Editors
Laura Buller
Jill Wiley

Art Editor
Keith Vollans

Production Controller
Tom Helsby

Managing Editor
Alan Ross

Editorial Consultant
Maggi McCormick

Publishing Manager
Robert Paulley

The Fotomas Index

Titles in the EXPLORING THE PAST series

READER'S GUIDE

Nick Harris

Imagine that you owned a time machine, and that you traveled back to the days when your parents were in school. Your hometown and school would look different, while the clothes, music, and magazines that your parents were enjoying might seem odd, perhaps amusing, and certainly "old fashioned" and "out of date." Travel back a few hundred years, and you would be astonished and fascinated by the strange food, homes, even language, of our ancestors.

Time machines do not yet exist, but in this book you can explore one of the most important periods of the past through the eyes of three people who made history happen. An introduction sets the scene and highlights the significant themes of the age, while the chronology lists important events and when they happened to help you to understand the background to the period. There is also a glossary to explain words that you may not understand and a list of other books that you may find useful.

The past is important to us all, for the world we know was formed by the actions of people who inhabited it before us. So, by understanding history, we can better understand the events of our own times. Perhaps that is why you will find exploring the past so exciting, rewarding and fascinating.

CONTENTS

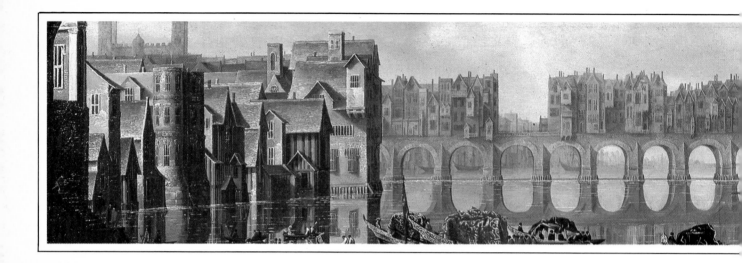

The Royal Collection

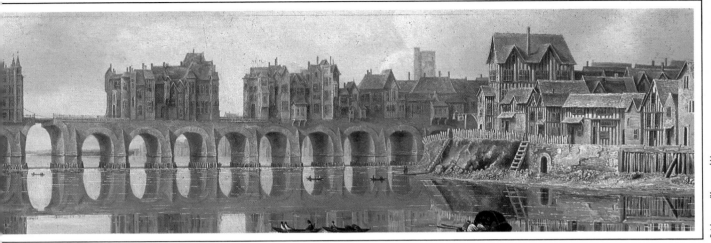

Bridgeman/Kenwood House

Mary Evans

INTRODUCTION

Graham Humphries

Mansell

Henry VIII, Elizabeth I, and William Shakespeare are among the most famous people in English history. Henry and Elizabeth—father and daughter—were powerful rulers whose decisions shaped the nation's destiny. Shakespeare was the greatest of all English writers; he expressed the spirit of the age in a series of wonderful plays that are still performed wherever English is spoken.

All three of these people lived in the 16th century, when America had only just been discovered. The world was opening up, and new ideas were sweeping aside the older ways of thinking. That is why the 16th century is often said to mark the end of the Middle Ages and the beginning of modern times. With about five million inhabitants, Shakespeare's England was only a small country on the edge of Europe, but the 16th century was a time of achievement. By 1600, England was rich, united, strong in national

feeling, and—thanks at least in part to her formidable fighting-ships—respected by other European states.

War and Peace
This success was particularly striking when compared to the weakness of 15th-century England. From the 1450s onward, the English King failed to control his powerful nobles, and there were bitter civil wars, known as the Wars of the Roses. At the same time, English people felt deeply humiliated by the loss of the wide territories they had held in France. Actually this was an advantage, since the attempt to keep the French lands had wasted England's wealth, and could not succeed in the long run. And despite the Wars of the Roses, English society was vigorous and healthy—ready to surge forward as soon as it was given peace and good leadership.

Except in the middle years of the century, these conditions

8

were provided by the kings and queens of the Tudor dynasty, who ruled England from 1485 to 1603. The first of the Tudors, Henry VII (1485–1509), ended the Wars of the Roses, brought the nobles under control, and enriched the Crown by careful management. Henry's efforts to make the royal government more effective were followed up by his son, Henry VIII (1509–1547), especially when the able Thomas Cromwell was the King's chief minister. As a result, royal orders were carried out even in areas such as the North and Wales, which had been hard to govern before because they were far away from London and communications were poor. English kings also ruled in Ireland, although their control over the country was very limited. Scotland, fiercely independent, was England's traditional enemy.

A Time of Change

Henry VIII was extravagant and tyrannical, but most English people supported him. They felt an intense loyalty to the Tudors, who had created a stable society, and they dreaded the possibility of new civil wars. This was probably one of the main reasons why they so easily accepted the religious changes introduced by Henry. Earlier in the century, Martin Luther, a German monk, had begun a revolt against the Roman Catholic Church, which until then had been the only form of Christianity allowed in western Europe. A rival form of Christianity, Protestantism, developed from Luther's actions, and Catholics and Protestants fought cruel wars against each other. England became involved when the Pope—the head of the Roman Catholic Church—refused to give Henry the divorce he wanted from Catherine of Aragon. An angry Henry rejected the Pope's authority and made himself the supreme head of the Church of England.

One of the most important results was the destruction of the English monasteries. Since they were very wealthy, Henry was able to take over large properties and vast areas of land, which he promptly sold off to his supporters. The monastery buildings were destroyed or converted into mansions, which is why so many historic English houses have names like "Woburn Abbey." A powerful, economically go-ahead land-owning class came into existence which had every reason to support the government and its religious changes. In general, the wealthy southern half of England welcomed the new order and was receptive to Protestant and other new ideas. The only opposition came from the North, which was poorer and more attached to "the

old religion." There, an uprising known as the Pilgrimage of Grace (1536) posed a momentary threat to the Tudor government, but it was half-heartedly led and savagely put down by the King's soldiers.

The death of Henry VIII was followed by a period of turmoil in which political and religious struggles were complicated by economic problems, such as inflation (rapidly rising prices). England became an outright Protestant country under the boy King Edward VI (1547–1553), then swung back to Catholicism under Queen Mary (1553-1558). English loyalty to the Tudors was shown after the death of Edward VI, when an ambitious noble, the Duke of Northumberland, tried to save the Protestant cause and his own hold on power by placing Lady Jane Grey on the throne. He failed because the country rallied to the rightful successor, King Henry's Catholic daughter, Mary, and the unfortunate Lady Jane—the "nine days' queen"—was beheaded.

The England of Elizabeth

A Protestant Church of England was re-established under Queen Elizabeth I (1558–1603), and her long reign made it

GOOD FRIEND FOR JESVS SAKE FORBEARE
TO DIGG THE DVST ENCLOASED HEARE
BLESE BE Y MAN Y SPARES THES STONES
AND CVRST BE HE Y MOVES MY BONES

J. Allan Cash

certain that Protestantism would be the religion of most English people. This fact influenced English life in many ways. Protestants believed that the Bible should be translated into the language of the people that read it, and so a Bible printed in English was placed in every church. The Bible and the Book of Common Prayer were the only books that most people knew, and repeated reading or hearing made them so familiar that their phrases became part of English speech. Another feature of Protestantism was Puritanism—a sober seriousness of outlook that affected many English people for several centuries.

When Queen Elizabeth came to the throne, her subjects hoped she would marry quickly, since hardly anyone believed that a woman could rule a country alone. Elizabeth proved them wrong, governing well, dealing shrewdly with foreign monarchs, and remaining determined not to marry. Her reign was gloriously successful, although full of dangers and tensions. There were plots against the Queen's life, encouraged by the presence in England of the Catholic Mary, Queen of Scots, and relations between England and Spain grew increasingly strained. But in 1587 Mary was executed, and the new Scots King, James I, was friendly, and the defeat of the Armada in 1588 ended the most serious threat from Spain.

The Spirit of the Age
In any case, the Elizabethans seem to have thrived on danger. Englishmen went out into the wider world as never before. They fought in the Netherlands, helping the Dutch to shake off Spanish rule. They attacked Spanish shipping and raided "the Spanish Main"—the silver-rich colonies of Spanish America. Some Englishmen went around the world with Francis Drake in the Golden Hind; others traded with half-barbaric Russia, wandered as far as Persia, and searched in vain for the Northwest Passage through Hudson Bay and into the Pacific.

At home, the same energy and enterprise made England prosperous. Land was farmed more efficiently, trade expanded, and the mining of coal and other minerals created new wealth. The population rose steadily, and London, with about 200,000 inhabitants, was already one of the largest cities in Europe.

All this helped to make England a bustling, confident place where many people were obviously better off. Thousands of sturdy new houses were built for gentlemen and yeomen (independent farmers). Grander, richer people—nobles, courtiers and ministers—put up spectacular "prodigy houses," such as Longleat House and Hardwicke Hall. Window glass, four-poster beds, drinking glasses, pewter ware, and other luxuries started to be more widely used. And food became more varied and interesting, although only the rich were able to sample the latest delicacy from America—the potato. Prosperity had its drawbacks, however, since large amounts of sugar could be—and were—imported, so that almost all English people, including Queen Elizabeth herself, had very bad teeth!

However, not everybody shared in this prosperity. In fact, many changes during the 16th century actually made the poor even worse off, and the government viewed the number of vagabonds as an alarming social problem. Because the Tudor police force was almost non-existent, people were harshly punished for petty crimes, or, if they could not support themselves, for leaving their home parishes.

A Golden Age of Literature
The new outward-looking spirit was shown by the increasing English interest in ideas from abroad. In Europe, the movement we now call the Renaissance was re-shaping attitudes to history, literature, the arts, and science. The Elizabethans were active translators, and they learned fast. In fact, with people eager to master subjects such as languages, good manners, courtly graces and statecraft, the Elizabethan period saw the rise of the do-it-yourself book!

In the arts, the English excelled in music, and above all in literature. Even if Shakespeare had never lived, the late 16th century would be considered a great age of poetry and drama. In addition to their priceless value as literature, Shakespeare's works give a vivid picture of his time; for example, of life at court (Love's Labors Lost), the risks involved in trade (The Merchant of Venice), the attitudes of the theater-hating Puritans (Twelfth Night), and even of seaborne exploration and distant places (The Tempest).

The Tudor dynasty came to an end with the death of Queen Elizabeth in 1603. Shakespeare lived for another thirteen years, into a new period that turned out to be as significant and turbulent in its own way as the age of Shakespeare's England.

Coll. Duke of Buccleuch/John Oritz the Elder

Henry VIII

P hysically huge and gorgeously dressed, Henry VIII stares boldly out of Hans Holbein's famous portraits. Even today, the image of the King is impressive and unmistakable. Henry's marriage problems helped transform his country into the land that Shakespeare knew. England became a Protestant country and the monasteries, for so long an important part of everyday life, gave way to a class of dynamic, secular land-owners. Historians still debate Henry's precise role in these changes, but to his subjects, Henry was a great king who dominated his country, his court and his times.

Tony Masero

Henry began as "Bluff King Hal," but his search for a successor soured his nature and his kingdom.

Personal Profile

HENRY VIII
Born *June 28, 1491.*
Died *January 28, 1547.*
Reign *1509–1547.*
Parents *King Henry VII and Elizabeth of York.*
Personal appearance *Almost six feet tall with stocky, athletic frame, later ruined by excess eating and drinking. Close-set eyes.*
General *A man of learning, who never stopped worrying about the nature of religion. His early love of life gave way to suspicion and distrust, and he became tyrannical and ruthless. Pain from his leg ulcer did away with exercise, making him fat and irritable.*

Henry Tudor, second son of King Henry VII and Elizabeth of York, came to the throne of England in 1509. He was an 18 year-old prince, a young man with fortune on his side, who, for seven years, had calmly anticipated his rule. He was the most handsome royal figure in Europe, splendidly dressed, almost six feet tall and built like an athlete. Indeed, young Henry was a renowned sportsman of his day and excelled at horsemanship, jousting, hand-to-hand fighting, wrestling, hunting and "real" tennis (a game like modern squash).

Aldus Archives/Ashmolean

HENRY'S FAMILY
Henry is seated with his hand on the shoulder of his longed-for heir, Prince Edward. The boy's mother, Jane Seymour, who was never crowned queen, is seated on the right. At the edges of the painting are Henry's two daughters, Mary (left) and Elizabeth (right) both of whom became queen.

The Royal Collection

JOUSTING
(below right) Henry jousts in front of Queen Catherine at the Tournament of Westminster held on February 12, 1511, to celebrate the birth of their son. The baby died soon afterward. It was a fall at the lists in 1536 which injured Henry's legs.

GREENWICH PALACE
(below) Henry was born and spent much of his childhood here beside the Thames.

He was a scholar, too; and, to the list of his many outstanding talents, he could add that he was an accomplished poet, musician and songwriter, and a keen student of languages – including French, Latin and Greek. Above all, he seemed well equipped for kingship, because his careful father had made sure that he was prepared for the role after his elder brother, Arthur, the first heir to the throne, had died.

Ronald Sheridan

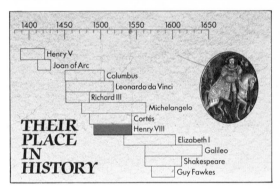

	1400	1450	1500	1550	1600	1650

Henry V
Joan of Arc
Columbus
Leonardo da Vinci
Richard III
Michelangelo
Cortés
Henry VIII
Elizabeth I
Galileo
Shakespeare
Guy Fawkes

THEIR PLACE IN HISTORY

Here, then, was a splendid man of the time—the Renaissance—and one who held every promise for a glorious reign over the quiet, peaceful England he had inherited. His people loved him, for his easy manner with the highest lord or lowest peasant further guaranteed his popularity.

But a cloud hung over Henry's court, and the following years were to see this magnificent prince degenerate into a brutal wreck of a man.

Seven weeks after his father's death, the new king married his brother's widow, Catherine of Aragon. The marriage was against all the rules of the Catholic Church, though the Pope reluctantly allowed it.

This was the fateful beginning to a problem that was to dog Henry's reign—the quest for a male heir to the throne. On New

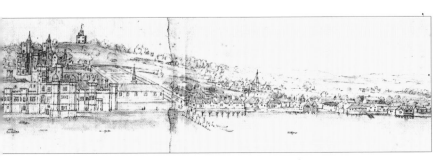

The Field of Cloth of Gold
June 1520

Henry VIII of England

Francis I of France

It was at the Field of Cloth of Gold—a plain in Picardy, France, between the villages of Guines and Ardres—that Henry VIII met Francis I on June 7, 1520. Those who saw the three weeks of feasting and jousting called it the eighth wonder of the world.

The two kings, accompanied by their huge numbers of followers, tried to outdo each other in pomp and splendor. Henry's glorious temporary palace at Guines covered nearly 130,000 square feet. The windows were framed in gold inlay, and the walls lined with silk. Golden statues of the Apostles stood in the chapel where the altar cloths were embroidered with real pearls. Outside, a gilt fountain spurted wine and water.

At Ardres, the French King's gold brocade tent boasted a roof adorned with astrological signs and stars made of gold leaf.

The glorious tented city in Picardy where the two kings met to celebrate their friendship.

Spectacular pavilions and arenas were erected for the jousting, dancing, mumming and feasting. Thousands of cows, sheep, lambs, chickens, herons and pheasants were brought in to feed the courtiers. But the French and English guests merely conversed politely during the banquets. They had eaten earlier in private—none of them wished to be poisoned.

Although everyone enjoyed themselves at this extraordinary event, nothing came of it. In fact, Henry was negotiating with Francis' bitter rival, Emperor Charles V, both before and after the meeting in Picardy. In 1521, Henry confirmed his support for the Emperor, signing a treaty for the marriage of Charles and Princess Mary, and for the invasion of France.

The war lasted four years; at the Battle of Pavia in 1525, the victorious Emperor took Francis prisoner. But he wanted nothing more from England, which he marked by rejecting Mary and marrying another.

Susan Moxley   The Royal Collection   Public Record Office

Year's Day, 1511, the queen gave birth to a son, and Henry and his court celebrated with jousting and feasting. But the "New Year's Boy" was dead by the end of February. The only one of Catherine's children to survive was her daughter Mary. Henry began to think that his lack of a male heir was God's punishment for marrying his brother's widow, which was forbidden in the Bible.

When Anne Boleyn arrived at court, the king was "struck with the dart of love." He became determined to be rid of Catherine, for Anne would not yield to his advances unless he made her his Queen.

From 1527, Thomas Wolsey, Henry's Chancellor, pursued "the King's great matter"—ending his marriage to Catherine. Henry argued that the Pope had been wrong to allow the wedding in the first place; therefore, the Pope should annul it.

Pope Clement VII refused. Wolsey failed and was stripped of his title. It was Thomas Cromwell who stage-managed the break with Rome. The Act of Supremacy, passed in 1534, confirmed Henry's own declaration that he was now head of the Church of England. Henry was then excommunicated by the Pope.

The marriage question revealed a dark and dangerous side to Henry's character. In 1533, Henry married Anne Boleyn. In September that year, the future Queen Elizabeth I was born. The king, angered and frustrated that he still had no male heir,

stayed away from Elizabeth's christening. Anne's two other pregnancies ended in miscarriages. Now, Henry's anger was lethal.

Anne was accused of treasonable adultery with five men, one her brother. Only one of the five, under torture, confessed his guilt. All were executed on May 17, 1536. Anne met the same fate two days later.

Henry's next wife, Jane Seymour, gave him the son he longed for—the future King Edward VI—but she died soon after (1537). The marriage of Henry to the young Anne of Cleves was part of Cromwell's complicated European diplomacy. Anne, intelligent but unattractive, lasted six months—Henry divorced her in June, 1540.

The young, lively Catherine Howard was married to the King in August, 1540. She was an outrageous flirt and was finally accused of being unfaithful to her royal husband. Catherine, like her cousin, Anne Boleyn, was beheaded. Only the dutiful and obedient Catherine Parr outlived the King; but, by the time of their marriage in 1543,

THE GARTER KNIGHTS
(left) The 26 knights, the inmost circle of the Tudor elite and "cobrethren" of the King, met at Windsor on St. George's Day to feast.

ROYAL PALACES
Henry constantly traveled between palaces. In winter, he usually stayed in London. In summer he traveled further afield to go hunting. Henry spent a fortune building new palaces, such as Nonsuch, Surrey (1). He also improved existing ones such as Richmond (2), Windsor (3), and Hampton Court (4) and (5). By the end of his reign Henry had 55 palaces. But despite their grandeur, they were often cold, uncomfortable places.

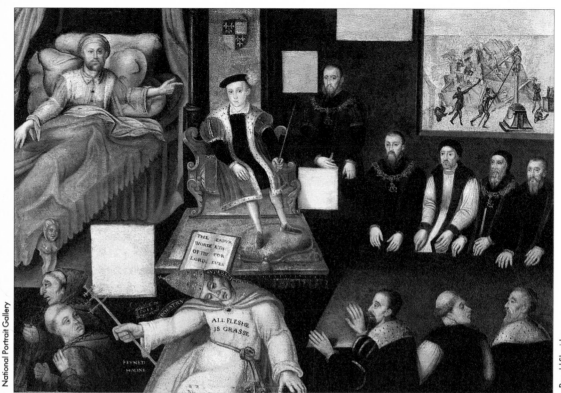

National Portrait Gallery

Ronald Sheridan

HENRY'S LEGACY
(left) A pointed snub to Rome, this picture was painted around the time of Henry's death. It shows the dying King naming his son Edward as his successor—and what was expected of him. Here, Edward is seen on the throne with the Pope at his feet.

Henry was a physical wreck. Feasting at Henry's court had become the scandal of Europe. In one day, the King and his courtiers disposed of 11 whole double sides of beef, six sheep, 17 hogs and pigs, 540 chickens, 15 swans, six cranes, 384 pigeons, 648 larks, 72 geese, four peacocks, 3,000 pears and 1,300 apples.

Not surprisingly, Henry had grown enormously fat. Also, he had fallen while jousting in 1536, and developed a leg ulcer that the doctors could do nothing to heal. In constant pain, he became more and more irritable and unpredictable.

London saw a royal reign of terror. "It is no new thing," said one visitor to the capital in 1541, "to see men hanged, quartered or beheaded . . . sometimes for trifling expressions construed as against the King."

Henry died, aged 55, at Westminster on the morning of January 28, 1547. On his deathbed, he directed that Jane Seymour's remains were to be placed alongside his at Windsor. His will named his children, Edward, Mary and Elizabeth, as his successors; and they all, in turn, followed him on the throne. But England spent more than a decade in bloody and bitter struggle before the crown was secure upon Elizabeth's head.

Michael Holford

MILITARY MIGHT
As a young man, Henry loved to joust and fight, and, as King, he longed to match his ancestors' success on the battlefield. So he had the country's armories built up (top) and spent a fortune refitting the navy (above).

LAST ARMOR
Henry's last suit of armor shows how huge he was.

The Royal Collection

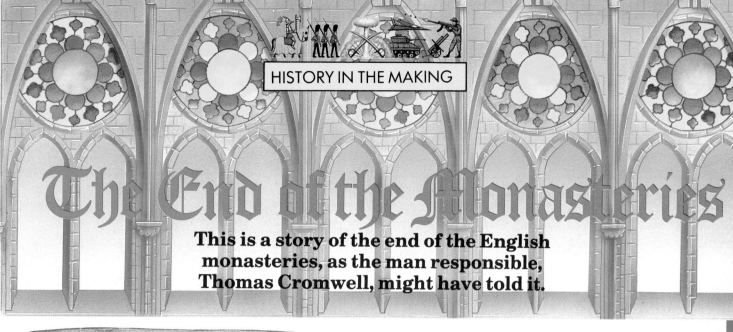

The End of the Monasteries

This is a story of the end of the English monasteries, as the man responsible, Thomas Cromwell, might have told it.

Henry, you are a fool! Tonight is July 27, 1540; and, when the sun rises tomorrow, I am to be beheaded. You could have saved me, yes—but you would not lift one of your great fat fingers to do it. I pray God will reward me better than you have done.

You cannot deny I have served you well. I have freed you once and for all from the interfering hand of Rome. I have broken the power of the Church and destroyed the monasteries for you. And, with their wealth, I have made you the richest monarch in Christendom.

Twenty years ago, you may remember, I was Cardinal Wolsey's man. It was Wolsey who was your Lord Chancellor then, not I. You deserted him, too, when he failed to secure your divorce from that stubborn papist, Catherine of Aragon, in 1529. If he had not obligingly died, no doubt you would have let Wolsey go to the block as well.

It was a dark time for me then, and I feared I might fall with Wolsey. But I called

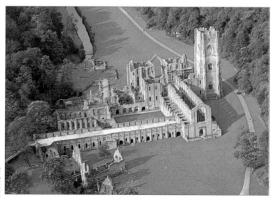

THE GREAT BIBLE *(above) The title page of the Bible in English, 1539.* **FOUNTAINS ABBEY** *(left) This Cistercian abbey in Yorkshire had 31 monks and an enormous income at the time it was closed in 1539.*

CARDINAL WOLSEY *(top) Henry VIII's first right-hand man.* **THOMAS MORE** *(center) upheld the Pope's authority and was beheaded.* **THOMAS CROMWELL** *(bottom) broke monastic power.*

17

in a few debts and managed to get a seat in Parliament. For three years, I worked to win your favor, and the allegiance of a large faction at court and in Parliament. That work cost me dear, but it gave me the support I needed to cow the papists.

By 1532, I was your first minister and had the Privy Council in my grip. It was then I began my work in earnest. Within a year, I had pushed through Acts in Parliament to knock away the power of the church courts and remove any right to appeal to Rome. That meant the Pope could go to the devil, and we could settle the divorce right here in England.

Of course, the Pope expelled you from the Roman Church, but by then we had the papists on the run. The next year, 1534, we made you head of the Church in England by the Act of Supremacy. A few years later, I commissioned a translation of the Bible into English and had a copy sent to every church in the land—so that our people might read the Holy Scriptures for themselves.

But with the monasteries still intact, the tide could always turn against us and sweep away all we had achieved. They were the living symbols of the power of Rome; and, while they remained,

CLOSING DOWN A MONASTERY

Graham Humphries · Susan Moxley

Bridgeman

END OF AN ERA
(left) A nunnery surrenders quietly to Henry's men.

Ronald Sheridan

POOR POACHER
Although corrupt, the monasteries had provided vital charity for the poor. Their destruction forced many poor folk to poach and steal to feed their *starving families —despite severe penalties.*

the clergy were not to be trusted. True, nearly all had acknowledged you as the head of the English Church—it was treason and death not to—yet we feared the Pope's hold on people's minds. The monasteries had to go, I knew. Besides, they were obscenely rich—my agents had shown they owned a third of all England's wealth—and we needed the money, for the wars with France had cost a king's ransom.

There was little love in the country for churchmen, then. The days when monasteries were centers of spirituality and charity were long gone. Too many churchmen lived a life of luxury and corruption, extorting taxes from the rich and poor alike, charging high fees for absolution and indulging in the worst vices. No wonder that many a poor man said he would rather meet a toad on the road than a man of the church.

By 1536, I was the most powerful man in the kingdom, but I needed concrete evidence of the monasteries' abuses. So I sent out agents to collect proof. They served me well; one wrote of the "vicious, carnal and abomin-

able living" in some of these so-called houses of God. When I read my report to Parliament, the chamber rang with cries of "Away with them."

It took me just four years to smash the monasteries; and, from 1536 to 1540, my agents traveled the land relentlessly, sweeping away the old order. The larger houses were all persuaded to dissolve themselves voluntarily—though I admit that the methods of persuasion were sometimes less than gentle.

To leave the buildings and their trappings intact would have been to invite their restoration. So my agents had orders to strip away all they could find—candles and chairs, bells and books, vases and vestments—and burn or sell them. The gold and silver went to the king. They then made the buildings unusable.

As for the monks, most were well treated and given pensions. Many became clergymen.

In 1539, Parliament ruled that the land and property of the monasteries now belonged to the Crown. A few schools were founded out of the proceeds, and six new

bishoprics set up. But the rest was sold to courtiers and merchants.

We spared Westminster Abbey, where English kings were crowned and buried. Tewkesbury Abbey in Gloucester was bought by the townspeople for £453. Dorchester Abbey in Oxfordshire was bought by one Richard Bewfforeste for £140 and left in his will to the local people.

Of course, there was some resistance to all this. In 1536, there was a worrying time for us, when thousands in the North joined the so-called Pilgrimage of Grace. We feared that papists across the country might rise up in rebellion. But, by guile and force, we persuaded them to surrender, and the abbots foolish enough to get involved were summarily hanged. In 1539, too, we were forced to hang the abbots of the three great abbeys of Glastonbury, Colchester and Reading. Yet I believe we have now won. The monasteries are gone, and so too have our most powerful church opponents.

But, as I have done my work, so I have made many enemies. And, this year, I made my first mistake. When I persuaded you to marry the German Protestant Anne of Cleves, I believed it would help secure the country. But your dislike for her has poisoned you against me. In an instant, you have forgotten all I have done for you, and my enemies have taken advantage.

Just seven weeks ago, I was arrested, and condemned without trial for heresy—me! Tomorrow, maybe you'll repent, and recall what I have done for you. But, for me, tomorrow will be too late.

THE HOLY ORDERS

Monks, friars and nuns lived in different groups, or orders. Most nuns, such as the Dominicans (1) led simple lives devoted to prayer and good works. Many friars lived simply too. The Franciscans (5) traveled the land like St. Francis, spreading God's word and begging for their food, as did the Capuchins (2) whose robes had pointed hoods. Many spent hours in study and prayer, like the Augustinians (3) and the Carthusians (7), whose order was very strict; while others spent time illustrating fine manuscripts like the Carmelites (4). The Cistercians (6) were great farmers, while Benedictine monks (8) were self-sufficient, even making their own wines.

Susan Moxley

ILLS and CURES

Today, we take the doctor's expertise for granted; but, in Henry's day, even a bad tooth could prove fatal.

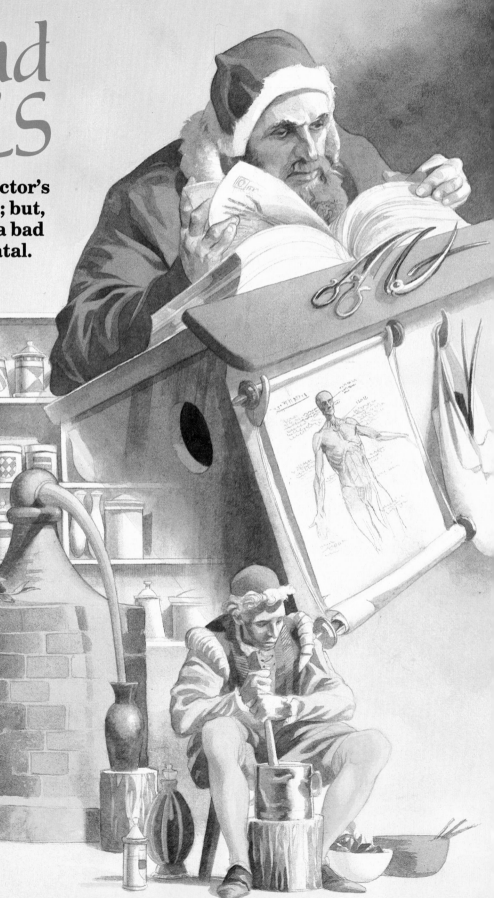

Fall ill in Henry VIII's England and you could be told to swallow powdered human skull, live buttered spiders, or crab's eyes. Or the doctor might prescribe "fustigation"—beating—as a cure.

Poor people in Henry's day relied on herbal remedies, but a heady mixture of superstition was never far from the scene. One such magical remedy was that a woman could be freed from her troubles if she threw a stone over the house where she lay—but the same stone had first to have killed a man, a wild boar and a she-bear.

Even the doctor's treatment could be bizarre. One highly respected doctor proposed this "cure" for baldness: "Shave the head and beard, and anoint the head with the grease of a fox. Or else, wash the head with the juice of beets five or six times, or else stamp garlic and rub the head with it; and, after that, wash it with vinegar." And if that didn't work, the good doctor went on to suggest honey, bitter almonds, oil of walnuts and

"such like oils."

Doctors in Henry's time believed that man's nature was made up of the basic elements of Air, Fire, Water and Earth. A "sanguine" man was a mixture of heat and moisture, Fire and Water, so his characteristic, known as his "humor," was blood. Phlegm was the humor of "phlegmatic" man, a mixture of coldness and moisture.

Any illness was the result of these elements being out of balance. The doctor's art was to restore that balance. Food, like all of nature, was also made up of the basic elements. So, the less brutal treatments had to do with diet: "The chief physic comes from the kitchen," ran a saying at the time.

Of the three branches of Tudor medicine, the physicians, who studied theory, formed their own college in 1518. Apothecaries, the forerunners of modern pharmacists, belonged to the grocers' guild. And surgeons were lumped together with barbers. The red and white pole outside some hairdressers' shops testifies to the bloody and bandaged history of surgery.

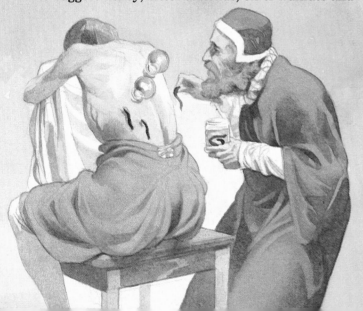

Nick Harris

23

Limbs were amputated and teeth pulled in the barber's shop, and alcohol, if the customer could afford it, was the only thing available to deaden the pain. In these dirty, unhygienic places, even a bad tooth could prove fatal.

It would be another 350 years before anybody knew about germs, or the importance of cleanliness. Soap was very expensive, and people rarely washed. One Englishman remarked that "the more the dirt is moved, the more it stinketh." Even kings and the nobility had to use perfume to cover their body smells. The common people could not afford such luxuries.

Most of Henry VIII's subjects lived in the countryside, where there was more room to dispose of waste and refuse. But the cities were growing, with perhaps 150,000 people in London, the largest. Only the main streets of any town were cobbled; and, in them, human waste and rubbish was carried in a channel at the side or in the middle of the road.

The byelaws of Chelmsford in Essex demanded, in 1564, that "every inhabitant shall scour and make clean the common gutter coming through the town, once every month." They added that "neither the butcher nor any person shall cast any horns, bones or any filth in the street or in the river there." However, at that time, there was little authority to enforce such local laws.

Most people died before the age of 50. At 35, they considered themselves old, approaching the time when "dried-up old age tires the body's strength." But at any time Henry's subjects could fall victim to ailments common in his day—fevers, jaundice, rheumatism, stones, chlorosis (the "green sickness"), worms "gnawing in the belly," quinsy or the "choking tonsil disease," coughs and agues (flu).

But it was the plague—the Black Death—that took the grimmest toll. The disease first came to England in 1348. It struck throughout Henry VIII's reign, in 1500–1502, 1520, 1527–1528 and 1535–1539.

A disease carried by fleas from infected rats, it thrived in the wood, plaster and

TUDOR FASHION

As Henry VIII tried to outdo the French in magnificence, the dull clothes of his father's reign went back in the closet. The new courtiers appeared in gorgeous, colorful costumes, studded with jewels and made from the richest fabrics.

Bridgeman

LADIES' COSTUME
The sketch above is by Holbein c.1540.

FRENCH FASHION
Henry's court was influenced by that of Francis I (left). Men's hair was short, and the embroidered French shirt was often worn.

Bridgeman/Louvre

SLASHING, *slitting fabric and pulling the lining through, was a popular style.*

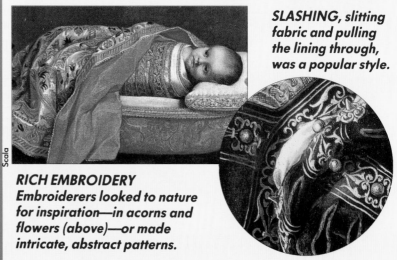

Scala

RICH EMBROIDERY
Embroiderers looked to nature for inspiration—in acorns and flowers (above)—or made intricate, abstract patterns.

MEN wore a doublet—a rich jacket of velvet or satin with puffed sleeves—and short, often padded, breeches (trousers), with stockings sewn onto the bottom.

LADIES wore skirts open in front to show the embroidered kirtle underneath.

straw buildings of the day. The one escape, only available to the wealthy, was to head for the country, away from the "corrupted" air of the city. A doctor wrote: "In such infectious time, it is good for every man to burn daily, especially in the morning and evening, juniper or rosemary, or bay leaves, or marjoram, or frankincense."

But, perhaps because it was less familiar, the "sweat" struck more dread. This disease of the lungs, accompanied by influenza, first appeared in 1485. Within hours, its victims broke out in a heavy sweat, developed a high fever and infected rash, and died. In 1508 and 1517, there were epidemics. In 1528, perhaps 40,000 people in London alone contracted the disease. Thousands died, and many who survived were so weakened that they fell prey to other infections.

The sweating sickness struck deep in the King's court. To avoid the contagion, Henry changed residences every other day. The doctors disagreed about treatment. Some recommended bleeding from the arm, from between the thumb and forefinger, or between the shoulders. Others suggested using herbal remedies, laced with molasses,

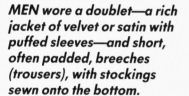

DOUBLE SLEEVES were highly decorated. The outer sleeve was puffed or padded; the under-sleeve was close fitting, with ruffs at the wrist. A huge variety of fabrics (right) was used.

JEWELRY, like these pendants (right), was worn by both men and women. Pearls and precious stones were often sewn directly onto garments.

Bottom to top: Scala/Bridgeman Art Library/Bridgeman Art Library/Scala

FLASH BACK

England at Work

SADDLERS (right) combined leather and metalwork to make fine saddles and bridles for horses. Like the blacksmith, they forged iron into spurs and stirrups.

Bildarchive Preussischer Kulturbesitz

Aldus Archives

Aldus Archives

WOVEN CLOTH WAS DYED in huge tubs (right) heated from beneath by fire. The dyes were made from natural substances such as vegetables.

GLASSMAKERS (above) made small bottles, tumblers and windows of great buildings.

Aldus Archives

ASTRONOMICAL CLOCKS (left) were made for the rich and privileged by highly skilled clockmakers.

Bilbarchive Preussischer Kulturbesitz

COOPERS made barrels for storing wine and salted meat.

WEAVERS (right) worked in their cottages on huge wooden looms, spinning wool into warm cloth.

Ronald Sheridan

sapphires, and sometimes pure gold.

Henry busied himself with study of the affliction. He sent herbs and advice to Cardinal Wolsey whose household was smitten with the illness. But it frightened him. The mere name of the sweat, said one observer, "is so terrible and fearful to his Highness's ears that he dare in no wise approach unto the place where it is noised to have been."

The 1528 epidemic hit a population already weakened by widespread famine. The staple diet of the poor was bread; and, if the harvest failed, there was starvation. The previous year's bad harvest had been followed by a severe winter. One week, the King had to send his own grain to London to prevent starvation.

The huge number of illnesses suffered in Henry's England led to a gradual recognition that society had an interest in health of its people. The first steps were taken in public health, in the form of health regulations. And medical science, because it was observing and trying to cope, however inadequately, was laying a foundation for the great physicians of later centuries.

Elizabeth I

L ike her father, Henry VIII, Elizabeth was a well-educated and intelligent ruler, but, as a woman, she could not rule her court by fear as her father had done. Instead, she transformed herself into a cult—the worship of "Gloriana"—and her courtiers became her permanent and worshipping suitors. The Elizabethan age was a time of achievement for England. Her ships fought the might of Spain, then the most powerful country in Europe, in the New World and defeated the attempted invasion by the Armada. At home, English culture flourished as never before, producing England's greatest playwright William Shakespeare, the "Bard of Avon."

Elizabeth I

"I know I have the body of a weak and feeble woman, but I have the heart and stomach of a king..."

With these words, Queen Elizabeth I gave one of the greatest speeches ever made by an English monarch. She was addressing 10,000 troops amassed at Tilbury Docks, near London, in August, 1588. It was a critical moment in England's history, for the invading force of the Spanish Armada was in English waters.

Since her coronation 30 years before, when this "indifferent, tall, slender and straight" young woman was crowned, Elizabeth had proved herself an intelligent and able ruler with a powerful personality. She had inherited the fiery temper of her father, Henry VIII, and she liked to have her own way. She hated for anyone to disagree with her, and often suffered convulsions and fainting spells as a result. Though well-educated, she could be coarse and swore a great deal. And while no one doubted her courage, many thought her to be cunning and deceitful.

As a child, Elizabeth suffered from the misfortune of being born a girl. Her father desperately wanted a son to succeed him as king and secure the Tudor family as the rightful rulers of England. Before Elizabeth was even three years old, Henry had accused her mother, Anne Boleyn, of high treason and had her beheaded. Shortly afterward, Henry remarried and declared Elizabeth illegitimate, debarring her from the throne.

Elizabeth was brought up in the country with her half-sister, Mary, 17 years her senior, and her younger half-brother, Edward, under the guardianship of Lady

FOUR FACES OF ELIZABETH, recreated to show how she might have looked aged about 13, 25, 55, and 65.

Bridgeman/Private Collection

Theo Platt

AT COURT
There was no Parliament as we know it today— Elizabeth ruled through audiences with leading statesmen who attended her court (right).

Margaret Bryan. She remembered nothing of her mother and saw little of her father, though he did allow her an education usually given only to royal princes.

Elizabeth was a clever, quick-witted child who was eager to learn. By the age of six, she could read Latin as well as English, and at ten she was studying French, Italian and Greek. Mathematics, physics, history, architecture, geography and astronomy were added to her studies in her teens, and she became fluent in French, Italian, Spanish and Flemish.

Like her father, who as a young man was one of the best athletes in Europe, Elizabeth loved exercise and sports. Her seemingly endless supplies of energy enabled her to continue riding, hunting and dancing even

Personal Profile

ELIZABETH TUDOR
Born *September 7, 1533, Greenwich Palace, near London.*
Died *March 24, 1603, Richmond.*
Reign *1558–1603.*
Parents *King Henry VIII of England and Anne Boleyn.*
Personal appearance *Above average height, slim with a fair complexion and hazel eyes, yellow-red hair, and bad teeth that turned black at an early age.*
General *Well-read in Greek and Latin classics, she was intelligent and witty, with a fiery temper and a sense of humor. Also rather vain.*

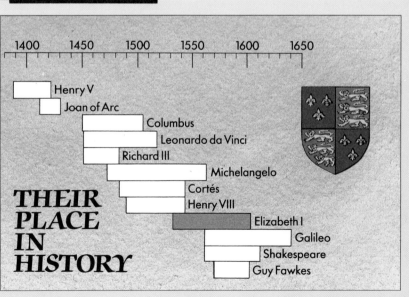

THEIR PLACE IN HISTORY

1400   1450   1500   1550   1600   1650

Henry V
Joan of Arc
Columbus
Leonardo da Vinci
Richard III
Michelangelo
Cortés
Henry VIII
Elizabeth I
Galileo
Shakespeare
Guy Fawkes

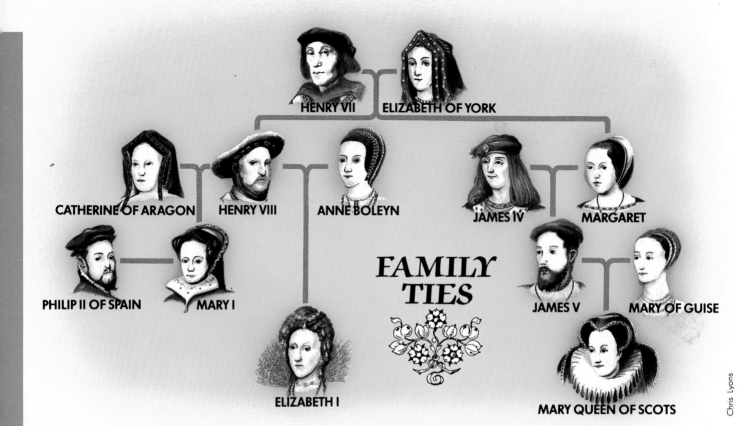

FAMILY TIES

HENRY VII — ELIZABETH OF YORK

CATHERINE OF ARAGON — HENRY VIII — ANNE BOLEYN

JAMES IV — MARGARET

PHILIP II OF SPAIN — MARY I

JAMES V — MARY OF GUISE

ELIZABETH I

MARY QUEEN OF SCOTS

Chris Lyons

into her later years. Five months after Elizabeth's 13th birthday, her father died. In his will, Henry acknowledged both his daughters, so that if his son, Edward, died childless, Mary would succeed him, and if she died childless, Elizabeth would become queen.

Edward was just ten years old when he came to the throne. Never a strong or healthy child, he ruled for only six years before he died of tuberculosis. However, the young king had been persuaded to name his cousin, Lady Jane Grey, as his successor. This unfortunate lady's reign lasted only nine days before Mary led a revolt against her and was proclaimed the "rightful" Queen of England.

Mary proved to be an unpopular monarch, whose cruel deeds in a time of bloody religious feuds between Catholics and Protestants later led to her being nick-

Michael Holford

THE OLD PALACE AT HATFIELD was Elizabeth's childhood home. As queen, she traveled from palace to palace, but Hatfield was her favorite.

THE QUEEN'S FAVORITE

Robert Dudley, Earl of Leicester (1532–1588), Elizabeth's favorite courtier and possibly the only man she might have married. Known as the "Virgin Queen," Elizabeth often said she was already married — to the "Kingdom of England."

Fotomas Index

The Execution of Mary, Queen of Scots

Fotomas Index

Mary Evans/Antonio More

February 8th 1587

In the early hours of morning at Fotheringhay Castle, Mary Stuart, cousin to Queen Elizabeth, spoke her last words. After a final prayer in Latin, the executioner's axe fell on her neck. It took two blows, some say three, to sever her head. And when it was held up, streaming with blood, a wig fell away, revealing long grey hair. Beside her corpse, her faithful little dog whimpered uncontrollably. So ended the turbulent life of Mary, Queen of Scots.

Born in 1542, Mary became "Queen of Scots" when she was one week old. Aged six, she sailed to France, already betrothed to the Dauphin—the future King Francis II. In 1558, they married and one year later she and Francis became King and Queen of France and Scotland. But the sickly Francis died and soon after, in 1561, Mary returned to Scotland.

Though highly popular on her return, Mary made the mistake of marrying a cruel and vicious nobleman—her cousin Lord Darnley. When Darnley was killed in 1567, she hastily married Lord Bothwell—regarded by many as Darnley's murderer. Alarmed by events, a group of Protestant Scottish Lords raised an army against Mary, and defeated her at the battle of Langside. Mary, however, escaped to England and turned to Elizabeth for help. But Mary was a Catholic and was thought by many English Catholics to be the rightful heir to Elizabeth's Protestant throne. Consequently, as a safeguard, Elizabeth had Mary detained. Mary was Elizabeth's prisoner for almost 20 years. Throughout, Elizabeth spared Mary's life despite being told that Mary was plotting against her. Finally when evidence was produced implicating Mary in an assassination plot, Elizabeth acted and signed the warrant for her execution.

named "Bloody Mary." As a devout Catholic, she lived in fear of being deposed by a Protestant plot. Believing Elizabeth to be involved in such a plot—as she may well have been—Mary had her arrested and imprisoned in the Tower of London for two months.

England breathed a sigh of relief when Mary died in 1558 and Elizabeth became Queen. The people hoped

that she would bring peace and prosperity to their deeply divided country.

During her reign, England did indeed prosper. There were no major wars until 1588, trade and industry grew, and footholds were established in America and India. But, while Elizabeth had proved that she could rule as well as any man, she was still a woman, and unmarried.

When she declared at her coronation that she would never marry, few believed her. But whenever she was pressed about the marriage question, she simply agreed to consider it—and conveniently forgot!

Whatever her reasons for remaining unmarried, Elizabeth was certainly not short of suitors. From the age of 16 to 56, she was involved in one flirtation or matrimonial scheme after another. She enjoyed the flirting and the flattery, but would make no commitment. Her childhood friend and long-time favorite, Robert Dudley, Earl of Leicester, once said, "I have known her since she was eight years of age . . . From that time she has always, invariably, declared that she would remain unmarried."

When she was 65, Elizabeth devoted her affections to Dudley's 20-year-old stepson, Robert Devereux, Earl of Essex. But Essex mistook Elizabeth's affections as weakness and took advantage of her. His treasonable actions proven, Elizabeth had no choice but to have her beloved Essex put to death.

RESPECTED AND FEARED

Though she was loved by her people and praised by such poets as William Shakespeare, she was feared and distrusted by her enemies in Europe. To the Spanish ambassador, she seemed "incomparably more feared than her sister." She was, he said, one who got her own way "as absolutely as her father did."

As she grew older, Elizabeth's vanity increased. She concealed her thinning hair with vivid red wigs, and covered her wrinkled and pock-marked face with thick white powder (she was a lucky survivor of smallpox). Yet she kept her slender figure and delighted in rich robes, studded with fabulous jewels.

Personal Effects

Elizabeth spent a fortune on her wardrobe, which included more than 2,000 dresses and items like this straw hat (which she wore in the garden), pairs of ornate kid gloves, and silk stockings—probably the first in England.

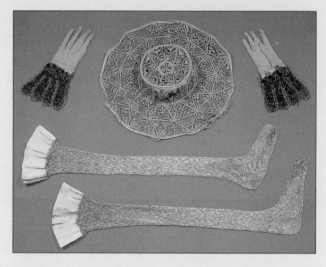

Fotomas Index

In time her voice grew "loud and shrill," she was very short-sighted and her manners, never elegant, could be crude. But her 44 years as queen came to be known as a "golden age," and she herself referred to as "good Queen Bess." Her death in 1603, at the age of 70, was the cause of great national mourning.

THE FUNERAL PROCESSION made its way through subdued London streets while all England mourned Elizabeth's death.

Bridgeman/British Museum

The Armada is Crushed

Spain's plan to use its mighty Armada to invade England was devastatingly smashed by the tactics of Elizabeth's fleet.

Philip II of Spain

Michael Holford/Prado

Admiral Medina Sidonia

Arxiu Mas

Elizabeth I of England

Bridgeman/Private Collection

Admiral Howard

National Portrait Gallery

On the morning of July 19, 1588, a huge fleet of warships was sighted off the Lizard in Cornwall, in southwest England. Formed in a majestic crescent, it turned into the Channel and bore down on Plymouth. On hill tops across southern England, huge bonfires were set alight, one after another. These beacons signaled the long-awaited arrival of the mighty Spanish Armada. The battle for England was about to begin.

That afternoon, a lookout rushed to report the news to Sir Francis Drake, Vice-Admiral of the English fleet, who was playing bowls on Plymouth Hoe. In this hour of supreme national crisis, so the legend goes, Drake remained cool and calm. "We have time enough to finish the game," he stated, "and beat the Spaniards, too!" With that, he went back to his game.

"We have time enough to finish the game and beat the Spaniards, too!" Sir Francis Drake

Art Gallery of New South Wales

Drake had no reason to feel so confident. The Armada was awesome. There were 130 ships in all, including 64 huge galleons. They were manned by some 8,000 sailors, while about 19,000 soldiers waited to do battle after grappling and boarding the enemy ships. Drake's superior, Lord Howard of Effingham, remarked that "All the world never saw such a force." Another observer thought the sea "groaned beneath the weight."

The purpose of this mighty force was to do no less than conquer England and topple Elizabeth from her throne. For years, this Protestant queen had been a thorn in the flesh of Philip II of Spain. His Catholic domains in the Low Countries (the Netherlands and Belgium) were under threat from Protestant rebels, and Elizabeth was openly giving them aid. And she was allowing Drake to plunder Spanish treasure ships in the New World. The Spanish nicknamed Drake *El Draque* (The Dragon), and they feared him as they would a mythical beast. But now it was time to bring this heretic queen and all her unruly subjects to heel, and the "invincible" Armada was Philip's chosen weapon.

"The Enterprise of England," as Philip called it,

THE BATTLE OF GRAVELINES

HOW THE FLEETS COMPARED

ENGLAND		SPAIN
102	ships	130
14,385	sailors	8,050
1,540	soldiers	18,973
1,972	cannon (over 4-pounders)	1,124
14,677lb	cannon shot thrown	19,369lb

Steve Biesty

Mary Evans/Charles Dixon

BATTLE OF THE GIANTS *At one point, the flagships of both sides, the* San Martin *and the* Ark Royal *engaged. The Spanish ship took a terrific pounding, but survived.*

involved a bold strategy. The plan was for the Armada to sail up the Channel in such strength that the English navy would not dare provoke a full-scale battle. Then, at Calais, it would meet a large Spanish army commanded by the Duke of Parma in the Netherlands. With the

English standing helplessly by, the Armada would then ferry this army across the Channel and that would pretty quickly be the end of the matter—the end of England, in fact.

To begin with, things went more or less according to plan. The English had about 50 ships—half their fleet—at Plymouth, but there was nothing they could do to halt the Armada's advance. Howard and Drake got their ships nicely into position behind the enemy, which meant they could pound away at the flanks of the ships with hit-and-run tactics, but no more than that. For nine days, the Armada moved majestically toward its destination, with the English snapping at its heels like a pack of terriers.

DISASTER LOOMS

The Duke of Medina Sidonia, commander of the Armada, was pleased enough as he anchored off Calais. He was where he was supposed to be, and he had got there with relatively few losses. Now, it was just a matter of meeting up with the Duke of Parma's army. Then, everything began to go terribly wrong for Medina Sidonia. He was informed that Parma's army, 30 miles away at Dunkirk, could not possibly come out to join the Armada without escort ships—and he had none.

While Medina Sidonia pondered this gloomy news, the English struck a shattering blow. At midnight on August 7, they packed eight ships with exploding cannon and inflammables, set them alight and launched them straight downwind at the Armada. This threw the Spanish into terrible confusion. They cut their cables in a desperate attempt to escape from the fire-ships, and

CANNON AND GUNCREW *More than 20 types of cannon were used on ships—from "popguns" to huge ship-killers which fired 30lbs shot. They were built either with a one-piece cast barrel, or with a breeched, built-up barrel on a stock carriage, as shown here (1). To load the gun, a measure of powder was put into the breech (2) with a ladle (3), a ball (4) rolled into the barrel and the breech refitted. This was secured with a wedge (5) and mallet (6). Side-to-side aim was controlled with a lever (7), placed under the stock to swing the gun around. The cannon was fired by igniting powder in the breech touch-hole with a lighted linstock (8).*

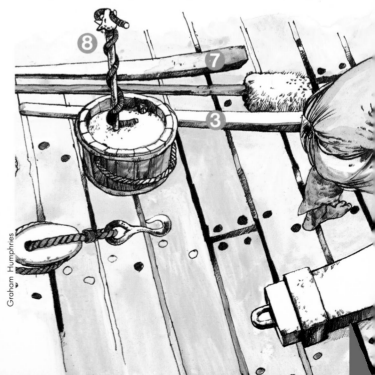

Graham Humphries

then began to drift before the wind. The great galleons began crashing into one another as the panic mounted.

At daybreak, the English moved in for the kill. In their lighter, faster ships, Drake and his men wheeled around the scattered ships, pounding them with deadly cannon fire. All day, the battle raged off the coast at Gravelines. The Spanish suffered terribly. Cannon balls smashed through the sides and superstructure of once proud galleons, tearing their sails and rigging to shreds. Sailors fell screaming to the deck, mangled by shot and sliced open by flying splinters. Dead and dying men lay everywhere, and blood poured through the Spanish ships' gun hatches and scuppers.

The English sailors sensed a victory. It could only be a matter of time before the hated enemy would be utterly destroyed. Then fate intervened. A sudden gust of wind separated the two fleets, giving the Spanish a desperately needed breathing space. But, to their horror, they saw that they were drifting before the wind in an easterly direction—toward certain destruction on the sandbanks of Zeeland. Then, at the very last moment, the wind suddenly shifted, allowing the battered Spanish fleet to slide by the deadly banks and on toward the open waters of the North Sea. The Spanish had been saved by a miracle—only to face disaster.

The Armada plowed slowly north, around the British Isles to the Atlantic and then home to Spain. It was a journey of some 2,500 miles, with shattered ships, wounded and diseased men, rotting supplies and slimy drinking water. Off Newcastle, most of the English ships—out of ammunition—had turned for home, leaving the poor Armada to its fate.

Many ships were wrecked on the stormy west coast of Scotland, many more on the even more treacherous west coast of Ireland. Starving, half-drowned Spaniards who managed to crawl ashore were butchered by the English and Irish. Fifty-one ships and 20,000 men were lost. Philip's great "Enterprise of England" had ended in the greatest possible calamity.

Manning the guns

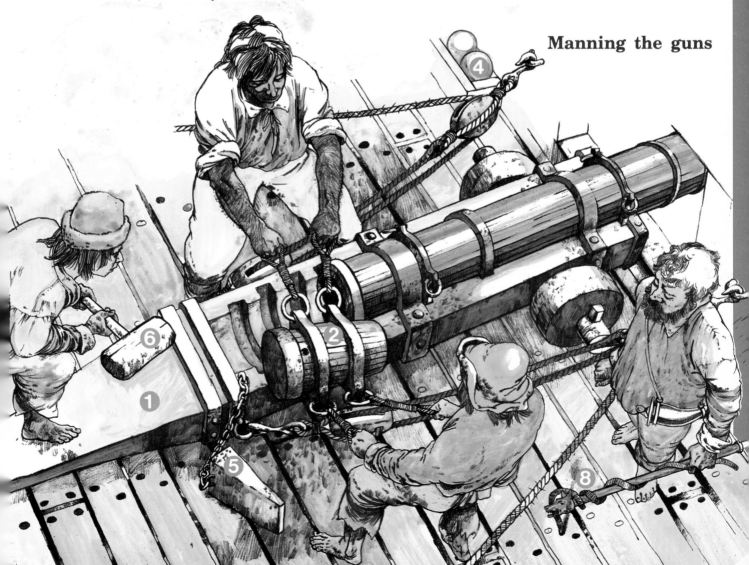

Elizabethan Life

**London—the greatest city in 16th-century
England—was the hub of Elizabeth's realm, but
city life was very different from today.**

At the height of Elizabeth's reign, London was one of the largest, most exciting cities in Europe—although it was only a fraction of the size of London today. Its population of about 200,000 lived and worked in or very near what is still called the City. This is the financial district of present-day London, the famous "square mile" facing the River Thames at its lowest bridging point.

To the west, London had spread as far as Charing Cross, and would soon swallow up the neighboring royal city of Westminster. On the other side of the river lay the bustling suburb of Southwark, while to the

Graham Humphries

east, new buildings were beginning to spring up around the medieval City Wall and the Tower. Beyond, in every direction, lay green fields and pastures. The Church of St. Martin-in-the-Fields, for example, now in Trafalgar Square in the heart of London, then really *was* "in the fields"—surrounded by grazing sheep and cattle.

Small though it may have been by today's standards, London drew people like a magnet. From all over Elizabeth's realm and beyond they came: courtiers seeking royal favors, merchants seeking business,

STREETS OF LONDON
In 16th-century London, the filthy and foul-smelling, narrow, winding streets were awash with sewage. Slops were flung out of windows, and animals jostled with passersby.

tradesmen seeking a living, actors and playwrights seeking fame, young people seeking adventure. And, of course, scoundrels seeking easy pickings.

London's main street was not a street at all, but the River Thames itself. It was alive with traffic—fishing boats, painted barges, merchant ships and shallow rowing boats called "wherries," the Elizabethan equivalent of the famous black London taxi, whisking people from one part of town to another. Their "drivers" enjoyed shooting the dangerous currents under Old London Bridge, much to their passengers' alarm!

In those days, Old London Bridge was the only bridge spanning the Thames, and it was nothing like any of the bridges today. It was jammed with high, narrow buildings—equivalent to today's apartment houses—which carts, animals and people had to squeeze between.

The center of fashionable London life was St. Paul's. This magnificent Gothic cathedral completely dominated London's skyline until it was destroyed in the Great

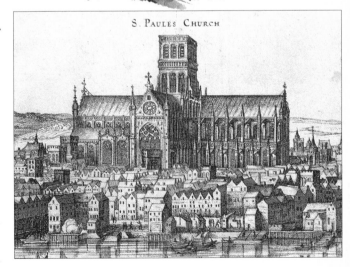

S. PAULES CHURCH

Bridgeman/Guildhall

ST. PAUL'S CATHEDRAL was the biggest building by far in London and dominated the capital's skyline. It was a popular meeting place for people of all classes.

FLASH BACK

Images of the Age

Piece of eight (Spanish)

Sovereign

Groat

Before the days of toothbrushes, people cleaned their teeth with mallow root or linen. The rich often used ornate toothpicks (above right).

High-value coins, like these, were made of precious metals: there was no paper money (left).

Among popular pastimes were music and board games like checkers, played on decorative boards (below right). Here, the lady plays a lute and the man an early type of viol (below).

Michael Holford/V & A

Mansell Collection

Bridgeman

Sir Walter Raleigh introduced tobacco to the Elizabethans—this fanciful painting (above) shows his first smoke.

Bridgeman/Kenwood House

Bridgeman/Gilling Castle

Bridgeman/V & A

LONDON BRIDGE was one of the most striking features of the city. It burned down in the Great Fire of 1666. In those times, as the old map (inset) shows, it was the only

Surgical instruments (above): 1 Tooth-puller 2 Amputating saw 3 Forceps 4 Hand-drill.

Barber-surgeons carried out amputations without using anesthetic—many patients simply died of shock (left)!

The poor wore homespun clothes, like this woolen hat. The shoes are leather (below).

Chris Lyon

Museum of London

Fire of 1666. It was every bit as imposing as Sir Christopher Wren's later masterpiece, and it was far more than just a place of worship. Londoners of every rank, from the highest to the lowest, gathered around St. Paul's to meet their friends, shop and do a bit of business. The central aisle of the nave was popularly known as "Paul's Walk." There, fashionable young men known as "gulls" paraded up and down, showing off their finery and hoping to catch up on the latest gossip. Shopkeepers set up stands inside, using tombs and the font as counters!

Stretching away from the great cathedral and the sumptuous townhouses of the wealthy along the Thames was a maze of narrow, twisted streets. The rickety overhanging house fronts made them constantly dark, and they reeked of garbage and human excrement. Sewage was simply dumped in the streets, and the City Scavengers carted it away to rubbish dumps on the outskirts. Foul-smelling butcher's waste—blood and entrails—was dumped in the river.

This careless attitude to hygiene was typical of the age. Rich and poor alike had little interest in bathing, so stench was just an accepted fact of life. So were terrible outbreaks of disease—like the plague, cholera and smallpox. And medical treatment was little better than nothing—if not worse. Barbers and surgeons were often

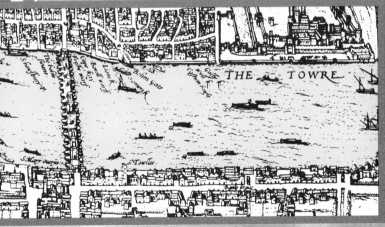

Fotomas Index

bridge spanning the River Thames. Its many supporting piers slowed down the river's flow so much that the Thames often used to freeze over upstream during winter.

one and the same, since the barber's sharp tools were useful for amputating limbs!

This rough and ready attitude to human suffering did not stop with filth and disease. London's poky, badly-lit streets were home to every kind of criminal—murderers, muggers, known as cut-purses, shoplifters and more. There were even schools for pickpockets and gamblers which were always bursting at the seams. Conviction for most petty, as well as serious, crimes usually meant a swift trip to the hangman's noose at Tyburn (now Marble Arch), or the executioner's block. Public executions were hugely popular, and the gruesome severed heads of victims were displayed on spikes.

Entertainments like bull-baiting, cock-fighting and bear-baiting were just as popular as public executions. Like hanging, they too had their own special place, in Southwark, right next door to Shakespeare's Globe Theater. A modern theatergoer would consider it shocking to watch a performance of *The Merchant of Venice*, and then saunter along to the bullring and bear garden to watch savage dogs tearing great chunks out of enraged beasts. But Queen Elizabeth saw nothing strange in these everyday features of her London.

FLASH BACK

ELIZABETHAN TRANSPORT

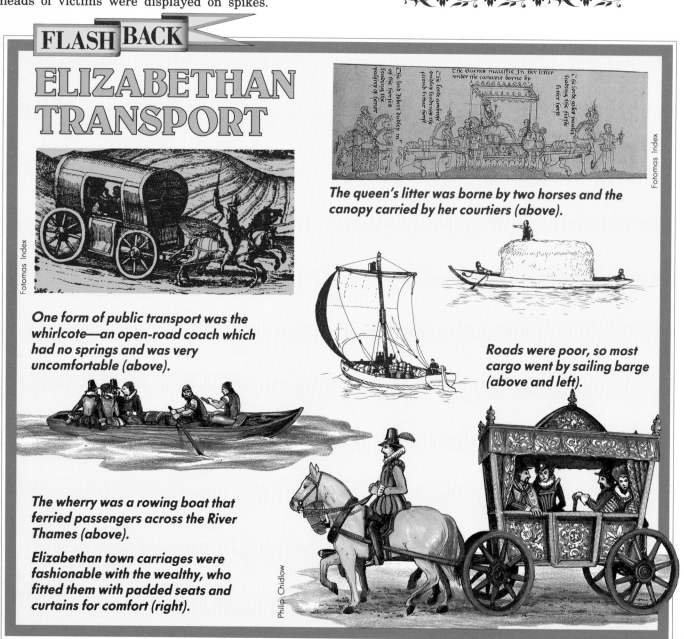

The queen's litter was borne by two horses and the canopy carried by her courtiers (above).

One form of public transport was the whirlcote—an open-road coach which had no springs and was very uncomfortable (above).

Roads were poor, so most cargo went by sailing barge (above and left).

The wherry was a rowing boat that ferried passengers across the River Thames (above).

Elizabethan town carriages were fashionable with the wealthy, who fitted them with padded seats and curtains for comfort (right).

Philip Chidlow

William Shakespeare

lthough Shakespeare lived on into the reign of Elizabeth's successor, James I, he was a product of the Elizabethan age. The Renaissance had little influence on English painting and sculpture, but the reign of Elizabeth produced some of the country's greatest composers and playwrights. Thomas Tallis and William Byrd wrote some of their most beautiful music for the newly-established Anglican Church. At the same time, English drama came of age in the plays of William Shakespeare, whose powerful language and insights into human nature mean that his plays are performed as often today as when he wrote them for London's Globe Theater.

Tony Masero

Known as "the Bard," William Shakespeare is regarded as the greatest English playwright of all.

So extraordinarily rich and full of life are Shakespeare's plays that many people feel that his life, too, must have been rather extraordinary. Some say he was really a wealthy earl who wrote the plays secretly for political reasons. Others say that he was Christopher Marlowe—a brilliant Elizabethan playwright who died young. But most agree that Shakespeare was Shakespeare, and that he was an ordinary, though remarkably gifted, man.

Few eyewitness reports of him survive, but the writer Henry Chettle described him as "very civil in demeanor, upright and honest," as well as a graceful writer and an excellent actor. Most pictures of him show a pleasant, kindly man. Only one, by a fellow actor, Richard Burbage, hints at something darker and more mysterious.

SCHOOLDAYS Shakespeare learned Latin from Lily's Grammar (below center) and Greek in the schoolroom (below). He did not seem to enjoy his long hours at school and probably preferred country sports.

J. Allan Cash

Mansell

Personal Profile

WILLIAM SHAKESPEARE
Baptized *April 26, 1564 in Stratford-upon-Avon, Warwickshire, England.*
Died *April 23, 1616 in Stratford-upon-Avon.*
Parents *John Shakespeare, glove-maker and alderman of Stratford-upon-Avon, and Mary Arden, daughter of a Warwickshire landowner.*
Personal appearance *Dark-haired, probably receding in middle age, with a high forehead and distinctive, classical nose.*
General *An educated man, honest, with gentle, courteous manners. Reserved, extremely discreet, cautious with money and conservative in his views. Respected as an actor and a writer.*

BEFORE THE QUEEN
Shakespeare joined a company of actors. During the Twelve Days of Christmas, these actors would perform at the palace. It was here that Shakespeare learned about courtly life.

A COAT OF ARMS
(below right) was awarded to Shakespeare's father in 1596 and inherited by the playwright.

Royal Shakespeare Company

Shakespeare was born on April 23, 1564, in the thriving market town of Stratford-upon-Avon, Warwickshire. His "merry, apple-cheeked father," John Shakespeare, was a local man who had given up farming to become a glove-maker in the town. His mother, Mary Arden, was the daughter of a wealthy landowner. The street where they lived, Henley Street, was always dirty and full of dung from passing cows and horses. But John Shakespeare's business was doing well, and their house was a solid, comfortable brick and timber building—indeed, the house still stands today.

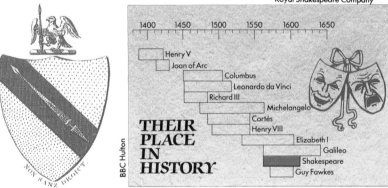

BBC Hulton

THEIR PLACE IN HISTORY

Henry V
Joan of Arc
Columbus
Leonardo da Vinci
Richard III
Michelangelo
Cortés
Henry VIII
Elizabeth I
Galileo
Shakespeare
Guy Fawkes

SHAKESPEARE'S BIRTHPLACE, *Stratford-upon-Avon (below), in Warwickshire (right).*

J. Allan Cash

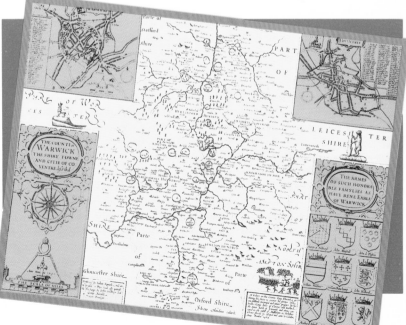

British Library

SHAKESPEARE
THE POACHER

✛┼✛

Coll. Duke of Buccleuch/John Criiz the Elder

Near Stratford-upon-Avon, there was a large estate called Charlecote Park owned by Sir Thomas Lucy. He was a wealthy landowner who kept game on his four estates. According to legend, young Will Shakespeare poached deer in this park and was caught by gamekeepers. He was brought before Sir Thomas Lucy, who was also a magistrate. He ordered that the young man be whipped. But Shakespeare, instead of showing sorrow for his crime, composed a satirical poem about his lordship, which began like this:

"A parliament member, a justice of peace,
At home a poor scarecrow, at London an ass,
If lousy is Lucy, as some volk miscall it,
Then Lucy is lousy whatever befall it."

This so angered Sir Thomas that he threatened Shakespeare with imprisonment—so Shakespeare, it is said, fled to London to escape his fate and to seek his fortune.

Royal Shakespeare Company

SHAKESPEARE'S PATRON, the Earl of Southampton, in the Tower of London.

By the time young Will was old enough to go to school, his father had become Mayor of Stratford. As Will sat studying at his desk in the old schoolroom, he may well have heard his father's voice booming out from the council chamber below.

Attending school was hard. William's lessons started at 7 a.m. in winter, 6 a.m. in summer, and finished at five in the afternoon. But his life would not have been all work. He may have rambled in the nearby Forest of Arden, or, with other boys, visited fairs and fêtes.

No one knows what Shakespeare did when he finished school, although one story says that he became a school teacher. Many an evening, though, he must have wandered across the meadows to Shottery, near Stratford, to court Anne Hathaway. Perhaps he wrote his first poems to her. He married Anne in 1582 when he was 18 and she was 26. Six months later, they had a daughter, Susanna, and in 1585, twins named Judith and Hamnet. Then, two years later, Shakespeare left Stratford to live in London, though exactly why remains a mystery.

The teeming streets of London must have

The Marquess of Bath

SHAKESPEARE'S RIVAL

This portrait is believed to be of Christopher Marlowe, the Elizabethan playwright and poet, and Shakespeare's contemporary. He wrote the celebrated plays Tamburlaine the Great *and* Doctor Faustus, *still performed today. He led a restless and depraved life and was also suspected of writing blasphemous pamphlets. One evening in a tavern, he became involved in a fight and was stabbed to death. He was only 29.*

been overwhelming for Shakespeare after sleepy Stratford. But if he was a little lost at first, he soon found his feet and joined one of London's leading companies of actors—probably the Queen's Company. Working for a company of actors was exhausting, as a different play was performed every day.

Gradually, Shakespeare began to help with rewriting old plays—adding extra scenes or changing lines to bring them up to date. Then, he began writing his own plays for the company. Even his earliest plays were successful, and audiences flocked to see them. By 1595, Shakespeare was the most famous playwright in England.

Despite his success, life in the theater was precarious. There were good times when the company performed at Court, or when Shakespeare and his fellow playwrights made merry at The Mermaid Tavern. But, there were bad times, too. For two years during the early 1590s, all theaters were

TITUS ANDRONICUS
This sketch from Shakespeare's play shows the Elizabethan idea of Roman theatrical costume.

PLAGUE
Plague was a constant threat in Tudor times. When it struck, people left London. In 1592, 11,000 people died and all the theaters were closed. Shakespeare turned to writing poetry for the Earl of Southampton.

Masters and Fellows, Corpus Christi College

Mansell

J. Allan Cash

AT THE MERMAID *(left) Shakespeare often met other famous playwrights at the Mermaid Tavern in London, and here they would talk "with subtle flame and wit." But their evenings were not always as refined and sober as this imaginary picture suggests. Often, they would drink and laugh rowdily, tell dirty jokes and chase the barmaids.*

closed when plague broke out. Then, in 1596, the Lord Chamberlain banned plays at London inns, where the company often performed. Forced out of their old theater, too, by a greedy landlord, Shakespeare and his friends made a daring nighttime raid on the decaying playhouse and carried away the remains to help build a new theater—the Globe—south of the River Thames.

Shakespeare continued to live and work in London; by 1610, he had written almost 40 plays. Perhaps at this point he thought he had done enough, for he returned to Stratford to live quietly with his family.

Shakespeare died in Stratford in 1616. He left most of his property to his family, but to the world he left many of the best plays ever written—plays still performed and enjoyed more than 350 years after his death.

THE MEMORIAL *(left), in Holy Trinity Church, Stratford-upon-Avon, overlooks Shakespeare's grave, on which a famous rhyme is carved (far left). He was buried here on April 26, 1616, exactly 52 years after he was christened in the same church.*

GOOD FRIEND FOR JESVS SAKE FORBEARE
TO DIGG THE DVST ENCLOASED HEARE
BLESE BE Y MAN Y SPARES THES STONES
AND CVRST BE HE Y MOVES MY BONES

The BARD'S THEATER

Mary Evans

OTHELLO, Shakespeare's tragedy, is about a proud Moor who kills his wife out of jealousy.

Mary Evans

BEATRICE AND BENEDICK are the lovers in the comedy, "Much Ado About Nothing."

Going to see a play at the Globe was noisy and exciting—very different from the theater today.

SHYLOCK, The Merchant of Venice.

When the yellow silk flag fluttered from the flagpole of the Globe Theater on the south bank of the River Thames in London, people knew a play was to be performed that day. The Globe stood out like a beacon above the low, narrow houses that lined the streets in this rather disreputable part of the city.

In Elizabethan times, playgoing had become enormously popular for all kinds of people, and the new generation of brilliant playwrights, like Marlowe and Shakespeare, had done much to make the new theaters that were springing up highly successful.

Of all the theaters, none was more popular than the Globe, a round wood and plaster building. The galleried walls were only about 30 feet high with just a few tiny windows, and the only way in was through a narrow door in a small tower. By noon on a performance day, crowds were already beginning to gather for the three o'clock performance, and soon the air was filled with shouts and cries as people jostled for a place near the front of the line. The theater held more than 2,000 spectators, but popular plays always sold out.

THE GLOBE THEATER, London, where the Bard's plays were first staged.

49

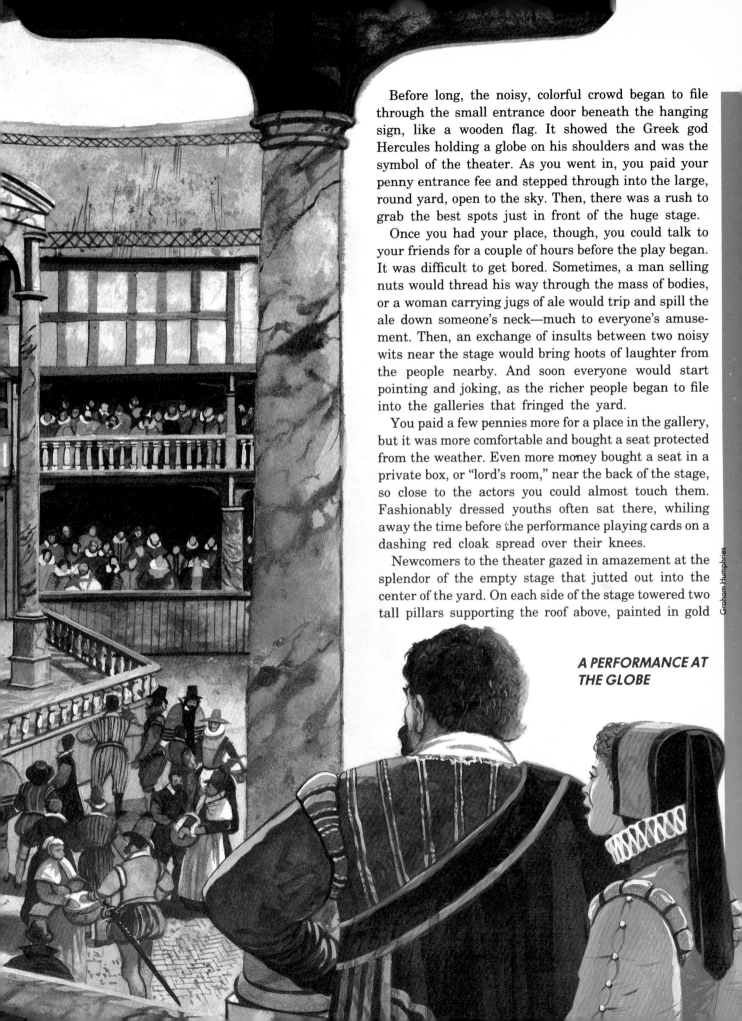

Before long, the noisy, colorful crowd began to file through the small entrance door beneath the hanging sign, like a wooden flag. It showed the Greek god Hercules holding a globe on his shoulders and was the symbol of the theater. As you went in, you paid your penny entrance fee and stepped through into the large, round yard, open to the sky. Then, there was a rush to grab the best spots just in front of the huge stage.

Once you had your place, though, you could talk to your friends for a couple of hours before the play began. It was difficult to get bored. Sometimes, a man selling nuts would thread his way through the mass of bodies, or a woman carrying jugs of ale would trip and spill the ale down someone's neck—much to everyone's amusement. Then, an exchange of insults between two noisy wits near the stage would bring hoots of laughter from the people nearby. And soon everyone would start pointing and joking, as the richer people began to file into the galleries that fringed the yard.

You paid a few pennies more for a place in the gallery, but it was more comfortable and bought a seat protected from the weather. Even more money bought a seat in a private box, or "lord's room," near the back of the stage, so close to the actors you could almost touch them. Fashionably dressed youths often sat there, whiling away the time before the performance playing cards on a dashing red cloak spread over their knees.

Newcomers to the theater gazed in amazement at the splendor of the empty stage that jutted out into the center of the yard. On each side of the stage towered two tall pillars supporting the roof above, painted in gold

A PERFORMANCE AT THE GLOBE

Graham Humphries

Music at the Globe

Music was an important element in Elizabethan plays. Three calls on the trumpet announced the start of a play. Music was provided by the theater's own musicians, who would set the mood for a particular scene, be it joyful, sad, solemn or something specific like a battle scene. They would also accompany songs and dances.

National Portrait Gallery

since the women were forbidden by law to act on the stage; young boys, about 12, played the female roles.

Because there was so little scenery, actors relied on words, costumes and special effects to create a scene. People loved noises and spectacles and came time and again to see plays like *Macbeth,* which had lots of action and violence, as well as witches appearing in a mist through the trapdoor below the stage.

There were other exciting stage effects. The noise of thunder and lightning was created by rolling a cannon-ball across a wooden floor. Loud trumpets and drums gave the impression of a battle. The most spectacular, however, was made from the "heavens" when an actor was lowered from the "heavens" onto the stage by a small crane. This machinery was housed in the "hut" which capped the stage; and, because it creaked, there was normally thunder, fanfares or music to hide the noise—which made the entrance even more dramatic.

It was not always easy to concentrate on the play, and playgoers were not very well-behaved. If they were bored, they might throw apples or oranges at each other or at the actors on the stage. Some talked loudly through the play or called for more ale and other refreshments, and most people thought it quite normal to make remarks about the actors while the play was in progress. Scuffles frequently broke out between groups of rowdy playgoers. Small wonder then that getting the attention of the audience and keeping them silent was no small task—far more so than it is today.

and bright colors to resemble the palaces of kings and princes. Underneath the roof, the "heavens" were painted sky blue and decorated with silver stars. At the back of the stage, on each side, were two doors; it was through them that players usually made their entrances and exits. Between the doors, a small alcove was hidden by a brightly painted curtain called the "discovery" area; during the play, actors could stay here out of sight.

Once everything was ready for the play to begin, a trumpeter announced the play with three loud calls. Latecomers hurried in and, for a moment, the audience was hushed. Then the actors stepped onto the stage to transport the audience to an imaginary world where all sorts of strange and magical things could happen.

There was very little scenery on the Elizabethan stage, but there were gorgeous costumes. Fine taffeta, silk, lace and tinsel in brilliant colors dazzled the eye; and soldiers appeared in shining armor, their swords and shields gleaming. All the parts were played by men

Dulwich Art Gallery

TWO ACTORS Shakespeare created Romeo for Burbage (above). (Left) Nathan Field took Shakespeare's place in the company of King's Men.

Mansell

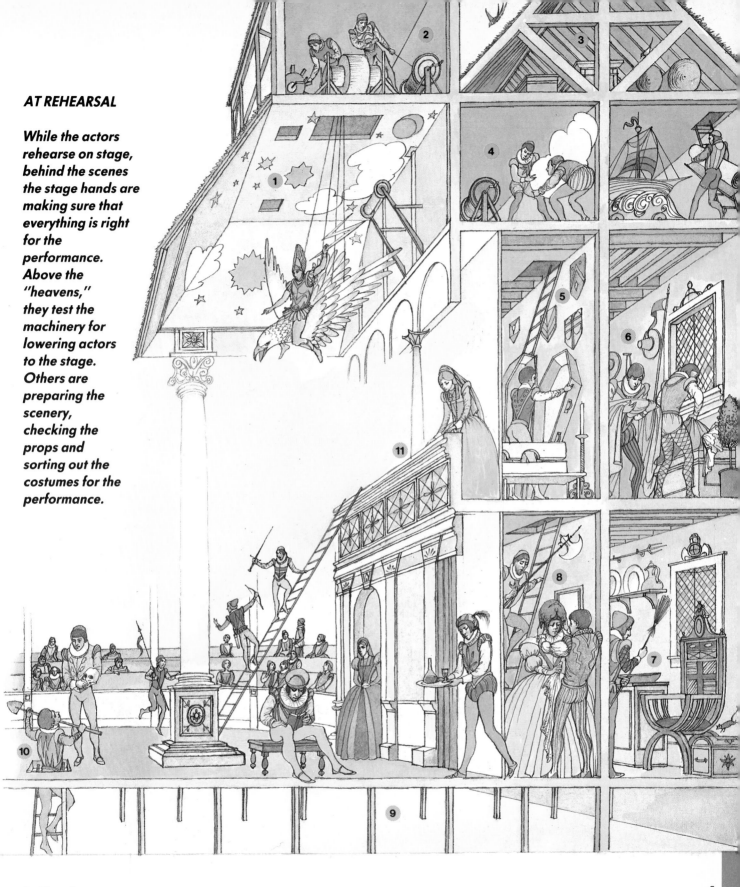

AT REHEARSAL

While the actors rehearse on stage, behind the scenes the stage hands are making sure that everything is right for the performance. Above the "heavens," they test the machinery for lowering actors to the stage. Others are preparing the scenery, checking the props and sorting out the costumes for the performance.

1   The "heavens"
2   The machinery for lowering actors to the stage
3   Storage
4   Pulley system
5   Props room
6   Dressing room and wardrobe
7   Props
8   Backstage (the tiring-house)
9   The "hell"
10   Stage trap door
11   Balcony

George Thompson

Making Merry

Fairs, soccer matches and bear fights made going out to play in Elizabethan times lively and, sometimes, violent.

Come summer, there were few things that Elizabethans liked to do more than visit the fair. Every town and nearly every village had a fair, and they were much noisier, livelier and more colorful than today.

On fair day, people would begin to arrive soon after sun-up to wander among the brightly colored stalls and take their pick of the entertainments on offer.

Exciting aromas of all kinds filled the air from early in the day. Cookies and pastries were molded into intricate shapes and decorated with gold leaf. Pigs and deer were spit-roasted over blazing open fires, and a few farthings would buy a tasty morsel. There were wrestling matches and tugs-of-war, too, and numerous side-shows. Among them, there may have been a "monster" show, where, perhaps, an exotic creature lately brought from abroad would be seen for the first time. And no

Elizabethan fair passed without a feast of music and dancing.

In town and country, rarely a week passed without the sound of pipe and tabor (a kind of drum). There were always fiddlers, too, and the more agile fairgoers would jump to their feet and dance jigs and reels. Occasionally, a rumor would spread that a dancing bear had come to town, and then everyone would stop what they were doing to watch this poor creature—often a veteran of the

POPULAR PASTIMES
Elizabethans could look forward to a host of traveling players who would pass through their villages and towns—masked actors, musicians, acrobats and tightrope walkers, a man with a dancing bear. At home, they amused themselves by kiteflying, archery practice, card playing, cock-fighting and, on May Day, dancing around the maypole.

Valerie McBride

55

bear ring—being put through its paces.

And then there were the Morris dancers. Dressed in brightly colored costumes, bedecked with bells and handkerchiefs, the Morris men danced and stamped their way through the streets. Sometimes, they would be accompanied by a hobby horse or dragon, whirling wildly to the music, twisting this way and that between the people—not a real dragon, of course, but men under an elaborate and exotic costume. Jesters wove their way through the crowds, tumbling and clowning and making everyone reel with laughter.

Important feast days were the occasion for special celebrations. The highlight of May Day was bringing in the maypole, a tall tree, chopped down in the forest and carried back to the village green by teams of oxen. It was decorated by the villagers with flowers and herbs twined around it in garlands. Flags and ribbons were tied to the top, and then it was set up amid great rejoicing while people danced around it.

Elizabethans loved these popular ceremonies; they were a great excuse for much eating, drinking, dancing and singing. The Puritans, however, thought that they were evil, heathen practices and, for a time, managed to restrict May Day celebrations. But when James I came to the throne they began again. James loved spectacles, firework displays and pageants as much as his subjects, the ordinary people, did.

COURTLY CELEBRATIONS

Inside the great houses and palaces where the nobility lived, merrymaking was very lavish. At Christmas time, in particular, the palaces of the nobles echoed to the music of the masque. Masque evenings were glittering occasions, when the great hall filled with flickering torchlight, and lords and ladies mingled with performers dressed in fantastic and gorgeous costumes. Silks and satins, cloth of gold and jewels, the reedy sound of the sackbut and the gentle jangling of the lute all gave a masque evening an almost magical feeling.

The masque itself was a succession of beautiful scenes with graceful dancing and soft music, often performed by the courtiers, who loved dressing up. With no limit on expense, the splendor of the scenery, lighting and stage effects matched the splendor of the costumes. The greatest architect of the age, Inigo Jones, made his name designing scenery and costumes for masques, often collaborating with Shakespeare's friend, playwright Ben Jonson, on masques for James I.

Not all merry-making was so refined, however, for Elizabethans relished cruel "sports" like bear-baiting

FLASH BACK

The Fotomas Index

REAL TENNIS (above), a cross between modern tennis and squash, was played on special courts. In winter, courtiers went ice skating (below).

The Fotomas Index

and bull-baiting. These, and many other, bloodthirsty sports were features of everyday life. Bear-baiting, in particular, was as popular as football is now. Bear rings, where the fights took place, were often built of wood and made especially for the occasion. But in London and large towns, they were permanent, much more elaborate structures, with galleries for the spectators—not unlike the Globe Theater. Even Queen Elizabeth had her own bear garden and proudly showed off her bears to foreign visitors.

Bets would be placed on the day of the contest as to how many dogs the bear would kill. Blood flowed and fur flew, as savage dogs were set on the bear, until the bear was finally led away, mauled and bleeding. Sometimes the dogs even got the better of the bear.

Queen Elizabeth's favorite sport, however, was hunting, and because the Queen liked it, so did her noblemen. Many country landowners had deer parks,

Royalty at Play

The Fotomas Index

COURT MASQUES
*(left and below)
Many courtiers
loved dressing up
for a masque —a
play with music,
fancy scenery and
costumes like these
by the famous
architect Inigo
Jones.*

*HAWKING, hunting birds with a trained hawk,
was thought of as a very courtly skill, and many a
royal lady liked to go a-hawking with her retinue.*

Mansell

REVELS
*Many dukes and
princes paid for
professional
theater companies
to perform plays
and revels in their
homes. Particularly
popular during the
Twelve Days of
Christmas were the
mummers—masked
players who
performed in mime.*

57

FLASH BACK

FUN FOR ALL

BEAR-BAITING (below) was a cruel sport in which a tethered bear had to fight off savage dogs. Bear gardens and theaters often stood side by side.

CHESS (above) was a pastime enjoyed by the nobility. This picture, from an instruction book dated 1614, shows the players choosing who will start the game.

*If on your man you light
The first draught shall you play,
If not tis mine by right
At first to lead the way.*

The Fotomas Index

SOCCER, a violent game in those days, was played with a stuffed pig's bladder.

The Fotomas Index

MORRIS DANCING (below)

FISHING AND HUNTING for the wild boar that still roamed the forests were both very popular sports.

Mansell

with wardens to look after them and keep out poachers. While the Queen's ladies watched the coursing of the deer from afar, the Queen herself preferred to ride with the men, carrying a heavy crossbow.

Hawking was another sport the rich enjoyed. Noblemen usually employed a falconer, who trained a hawk to fly from its master's gloved hand. With tiny bells tied to its legs, the hawk was released to pursue birds on the wing and taught to return with its prey.

While the rich enjoyed their hunting, hawking and the new game of tennis, imported from France, ordinary people played soccer. This was a violent game, with teams of unlimited size and almost no rules.

It had been played by the common folk for centuries, and in the past, there had been many attempts to ban it. Not only were men badly injured and sometimes killed, but fights often broke out between opposing teams. Just as today, the authorities believed that it caused riots and brawls. Merchants disliked it because it kept men away from work, and the ministers disapproved of it strongly because it was played on Sunday. But it helped the people to let off steam; and, like the pageants and plays that they liked so much, it took people away from the harsh world in which they lived—at least for a time.

GLOSSARY

abbot The head of an abbey or monastery.

absolution In the Roman Catholic Church, the pardoning of all sins.

abstract A design that is not a copy of natural objects.

affliction The sickness itself, and what has caused it.

alderman A member of a local council who is second-in-command to the mayor.

allegiance Loyalty and obedience to a king, government, or country.

Anglican Of the Church of England; in the USA, the Protestant Episcopal Church.

annul To cancel a marriage and declare that it never existed.

armada A fleet of armed ships.

aroma A smell, usually sweet and spicy.

bard A poet.

betrothed Promised in marriage, or engaged to be married.

blasphemy To speak disrespectfully of God or anything religious.

breech The rear end of a cannon, where the ammunition is inserted.

brocade A fabric that has a raised pattern embroidered on or woven into it.

contagion The spreading of a disease by contact with someone who has the illness.

Dauphin (French) The title given to the eldest son of the King of France.

debar Stop from entering, or exclude.

demeanor The way in which a person behaves, as seen by others.

depose Remove from a position of power.

domain The home or land a person owns or controls.

dynasty Rulers from the same family.

escort Ships that accompany other ships to give them protection.

excommunication The most serious punishment given by the Roman Catholic Church, which bans a person from having anything to do with the Church—including Christian burial—and its members.

farthing A small English coin that was worth a fourth of a penny.

font An eight-sided, stone basin that holds the water used for baptism.

galleon A large sailing ship of the 15th and 16th centuries, used for overseas trade and war.

gallery Covered passageway, open on one side.

Gothic Art style of the Middle Ages, especially referring to architecture. Pointed arches were a major feature.

heresy A belief, either political or religious, that is different from the ideas of the governing power, especially if that belief is thought to be harmful.

inflammable Something that catches on fire or burns easily.

jester An entertainer, who jokes and plays the fool.

jig A lively dance, particularly Gaelic, in which each person dances alone.

joust Fight on horseback, with a lance, against another competitor.

kirtle An outer petticoat.

linstock A pole that held a lighted match for firing cannons.

lists Two lanes, divided by a rail, down which two knights on horseback would charge at one another.

magistrate One who is given the power to enforce law and order; a justice of the peace.

Moor Someone of mixed Arab and northern African descent.

Morris dance Traditional folk dance, with **Moorish** origins, associated with May Day games, and danced by a group of specially-trained men.

mythical Something spoken of as if it is real, but is fantastic and unbelievable.

one-piece cast Made in one piece, by pouring liquid metal into a mold and leaving it to harden.

papist A Roman Catholic or follower of the Pope, but only used by people who are against the Catholic Church.

pock-mark The scarring or holes left in the skin after the blisters from smallpox have healed.

poky Small, cramped, and very uncomfortable.

precarious Insecure and uncertain; depending upon decisions made by someone else.

prop Any movable item that is added to the stage set, to give a realistic appearance. Abbreviation of "property."

Puritan A person who wished to change the Church of England, by "purifying" it of all ceremony; in general today, someone strict in morals and religion.

ramble A pleasurable walk, one that follows no particular path.

reel A lively country dance, in which two or more couples dance in "a set"—in two lines, facing one another.

rehearsal The private practice of a play, to help learn it, before it is performed in public.

revel Organized fun, with noisy feasts, dancing and entertainers.

rigging The ropes and chains that support the masts and work the sails of a ship.

Roman Church The Roman Catholic Church.

sackbut Old-fashioned musical instrument with a slide, similar to a trombone.

scupper A hole in the side of a ship that allows the water to drain off the deck.

superstructure The upper part of a ship that is above the main deck.

tavern A place where people went to drink alcohol—a bar or saloon.

trappings Ornaments and decorations.

vagabond A wandering hobo or beggar.

vestment Robe worn in certain religious ceremonies and rites.

Scala

CHRONOLOGY

Shakespeare's England 1500–1620

	POLITICS AND WAR	SCIENCE AND EXPLORATION
1500 to 1530	**1502** Arthur, Henry VII's elder son dies. The King's second son, Henry, becomes heir to the throne. **1509** Henry VII dies and is succeeded by Henry VIII. **1519** Charles of Spain becomes Emperor Charles V, the most powerful ruler in Europe. **1527** Henry VIII asks Pope to divorce him from Queen Catherine of Aragon. **1527** Imperial Troops sack Rome. **1530** Cardinal Thomas Wolsey, Henry VIII's chief minister dies, after having been arrested as a traitor for failure to obtain the King's divorce.	**1500** Florentine navigator, Amerigo Vespucci discovers mouth of the Amazon River. **1506** Christopher Columbus dies. **1507** The New World is renamed America. **1512** Copernicus publishes *Commentaries,* in which he states that Sun is center of the solar system. **1513** Spaniard, Ponce de Leon, discovers Florida. **1516** Coffee is imported into Europe. **1519** Hernán Cortés conquers the Aztecs. **1519–1521** Portuguese under Ferdinand Magellan first to sail around the world (Magellan dies during the journey).
1531 to 1560	**1533** Henry VIII divorces his wife, and marries Anne Boleyn; their daughter, the future Elizabeth I, is born. **1534** England breaks all ties with the Pope in Rome. **1536** Catherine of Aragon dies. Anne Boleyn is executed. Henry marries Jane Seymour. **1537** Jane dies after giving birth to the future Edward VI. **1540** Henry marries Anne of Cleves, but has the marriage annulled and marries Catherine Howard. **1542** Queen Catherine Howard is executed. **1543** Henry VIII marries Catherine Parr. **1547** Henry VIII is succeeded by only son, Edward VI. **1553** Edward VI dies. Mary, Henry VIII's elder daughter, becomes Queen. **1554** Mary marries Philip II of Spain. **1558** Elizabeth I, Henry's younger daughter, becomes Queen of England.	**1531** Rio de Janeiro discovered by Nicolas Villegagnon. **1531–1533** Francisco Pizarro conquers the Incas. **1535** Jacques Cartier sails up the St. Lawrence River. **1540** Hernando de Soto discovers the Mississippi River. **1542** Antonio da Mota is first European to enter Japan. **1544** Silver mines are discovered in Potosi, Peru. **1546** Geographer, Gerardus Mercator, describes Earth's magnetic pole. **1554** Sir Walter Raleigh is born. **1555** Tobacco is brought from America to Spain. **1559** Tobacco is imported into France by Jean Nicot. (Nicotine is named after him.)
1561 to 1590	**1562** English troops take Le Havre, France. **1568** Mary, Queen of Scots is defeated and forced to take refuge in England. Elizabeth I imprisons her. **1572** Francis Drake attacks Spanish-American harbors. **1578** King James VI takes over Scottish government. **1579** Francis Drake proclaims sovereignty of England over New Albion, California. **1587** Mary, Queen of Scots is executed. **1588** Spanish Armada is defeated. **1589** House of Commons appoints first Standing Committee for Privileges to defend itself against the power of the Crown.	**1562** French colony in Florida is destroyed by Spanish. **1564** Galileo Galilei, "father of modern science," born. **1565** Tobacco and sweet potatoes are imported to England by Sir John Hawkins, English navigator. **1570** Abraham Ortelius publishes first modern atlas. **1577** Englishman, Humphrey Gilbert, is given permission by the Government to found colonies in North America. **1577–1580** Francis Drake sails around the world. **1584** Sir Walter Raleigh founds first English colony in Virginia. **1589** William Lee invents first knitting machine.
1591 to 1620	**1596** English attack Cadiz, Spain, and hinder second Armada. **1599** English general, Oliver Cromwell, is born. **1600** The future Charles I of England is born. **1603** Queen Elizabeth I dies. James VI arrives from Scotland, to become King James I of England. **1604** Peace treaty between England and Spain. **1605** "Gunpowder Plot." Guy Fawkes arrested trying to blow up the Houses of Parliament. **1613** English colonists in Virginia destroy French settlement in Nova Scotia. French are prevented from colonizing Maryland. **1614** Virginian colonists stop French settling in Maine and Nova Scotia. **1618** Sir Walter Raleigh is executed.	**1591** James Lancaster leaves England on first voyage to the East Indies. **1595** Sir Walter Raleigh explores the Orinoco River. **1596** Galileo invents the thermometer. **1596** Sir Francis Drake dies. **1600** East India Company founded. **1600** Dutch opticians invent the telescope. **1607** John Smith founds colony of Virginia at Jamestown. **1609** Henry Hudson sails up the Hudson River. **1609** First tea is shipped to Europe from China. **1619** First African slaves arrive in Virginia. **1620** Pilgrim Fathers sail from England in the *Mayflower* to found Massachusetts.

The 16th century was a time of immense change for England. Protestantism replaced Roman Catholicism as the religion of the majority of English people. England lost Calais, the last remnant of her French lands, while her seamen began the exploration of North America that was to lead to the original thirteen colonies of the United States.

RELIGION AND SOCIETY	ART AND LITERATURE	
1503 William Warham becomes last pre-Reformation Archbishop of Canterbury. 1503 First English translation of Thomas à Kempis's *Imitation of Christ*. 1515 Archbishop Thomas Wolsey made a Cardinal and Lord Chancellor of England. 1521 Pope Leo X makes Henry VIII "Defender of the Faith" after Henry defends Roman Catholicism against Martin Luther. 1527 Henry asks Pope Clement VII to grant him a divorce from Queen Catherine of Aragon.	1503 Work begins on Henry VII's Chapel in Westminster Abbey, London. 1505 Thomas Tallis, English composer, born. 1509 Desiderius Erasmus, Dutch Humanist, publishes *Praise of Folly*, dedicated to Sir Thomas More. 1515 Hampton Court Palace begun for Cardinal Wolsey. 1516 *Utopia* by Sir Thomas More published. 1525 Wolsey gives Hampton Court Palace to Henry VIII. 1527 Hans Holbein the Younger paints *Thomas More and his Family*. 1529 English poet and dramatist, John Skelton, dies.	1500 to 1530
1531 Henry VIII is recognized by the English clergy as the Supreme Head of the Church of England. 1533 Henry VIII is excommunicated by the Pope. 1534 Henry breaks with the Roman Catholic Church by the Act of Supremacy. 1534–1539 Dissolution of the English monasteries. 1536–1537 Pilgrimage of Grace, an uprising in the North of England against the dissolution of the monasteries. 1539 Six Articles of Religion issued. They outline the beliefs of the Church of England. 1549 Protestant Act of Uniformity passed and the Book of Common Prayer issued. 1554 Queen Mary restores Roman Catholicism. 1558 Elizabeth I returns England to Protestantism. 1560 Beginnings of Puritanism. Followers of John Calvin wish to reform the Anglican Church still further.	1535 Hans Holbein paints portrait, *King Henry VIII*. 1536 Erasmus dies. 1536 Holbein made Court Painter to Henry VIII. 1539 Holbein paints portrait, *Anne of Cleves*. 1542 Sir Thomas Wyatt, English poet and admirer of Anne Boleyn, dies. 1543 Holbein dies. 1543 William Byrd, English composer, born. 1547 Earl of Surrey, English poet, executed for treason against Henry VIII 1548 John Bale writes *King John*, first known English historical play. 1550 Nicholas Udall writes *Ralph Roister Doister*, first known English comic play. 1554 John Lyly, English playwright, born. 1558 Thomas Kyd, English playwright, born.	1531 to 1560
1561 Thomas Norton translates Calvin's *Institution of the Christian Religion*. 1562 First English edition of John Foxe's *Book of Martyrs*. 1563 Thirty-nine Articles, which set out the beliefs of the Anglican Church, are issued. 1568 Archbishop Parker, with the help of English bishops, produces the "Bishops' Bible." 1570 Elizabeth I is excommunicated from the Roman Catholic Church. 1575 Edmund Campion and Robert Parsons return to England to begin the first Jesuit mission. 1581 Edmund Campion tried and executed for treason.	1564 Marlowe and Shakespeare born. 1570 Nicholas Hilliard paints portrait, *Queen Elizabeth 1*. 1572 John Donne, English poet, born. 1573 Inigo Jones, English architect, born. 1574 First theater opened in London by actor, Richard Burbage. 1577 Raphael Holinshed publishes his *Chronicles*, used by Shakespeare as a source for his history plays. 1578 John Lyly writes *Euphues*, first English novel. 1588 Christopher Marlowe writes *Dr. Faustus*. 1590–1609 Edmund Spenser writes poem, *The Fairie Queene*.	1561 to 1590
1592 New edition of the Vulgate (Roman Catholic Bible) published. 1593 Act is passed restricting the Puritans' religious freedom. 1603 Roger Williams, founder of the colony of Rhode Island and believer in religious liberty, is born. 1603 Severe outbreak of plague in England. 1604 James I and Anglican Bishops debate with Puritans at the Hampton Court conference. James commissions a new translation of the Bible. 1611 King James Authorized Version of the Bible published. 1612 The last known time that heretics were burned in England. 1612 Sir Francis Bacon publishes his *Essay* on "Atheism."	1592 Thomas Kyd writes play, *The Spanish Tragedy*. c.1593 William Shakespeare begins writing plays in London. 1597 John Dowland composes his *First Book of Songs*. 1599 Globe Theater built in Southwark, London. Many of Shakespeare's plays performed here. 1602 Bodleian Library opens in Oxford. 1608 John Milton, English poet, born. 1611 William Byrd, John Bull and Orlando Gibbons compose collection of music, *Parthemia*. 1613 Globe Theater burns down. 1614 Sir Walter Raleigh writes *The History of the World*. 1617 James I makes Ben Jonson the first Poet Laureate. 1619–1622 Banqueting House, Whitehall, London built. Inigo Jones is architect.	1591 to 1620

FURTHER READING

Mary Evans/Charles Dixon

Alexander, Michael V., *The First of the Tudors: A Study of Henry VII and His Reign*. Rowman & Littlefield (Totowa, 1980)

Dwyer, Frank, *Henry VIII*. Chelsea House (Edgemont, 1988)

Elton, G.R., *Policy and Police: The Enforcement of the Reformation in the Age of Thomas Cromwell*. Cambridge University Press (New York, 1985)

Erickson, Carolly, *Bloody Mary*. St. Martin's Press (New York, 1985)

Fletcher, Anthony, *Elizabethan Village*. Longman (White Plains, 1972)

Fripp, Edgar I., *Shakespeare's Stratford*. Ayer Co. Publications (Salem, 1928)

Garnett, Henry, *Know About the Armada*. Dufour Editions (Chester Springs, 1967)

Goodnough, David, *Francis Drake*. Troll Associates (Mahwah, 1979)

Harris Fair, Martha, *Shakespeare's Plays for Young People*. Harris Academy (Denver, 1982)

Harris, Nathaniel, *The Armada*. David & Charles (North Pomfret, 1987)

Harrowen, Jean, *Origins and Tales of London Town*. David & Charles (North Pomfret, 1984)

Luke, Mary, *The Nine Days' Queen: A Portrait of Lady Jane Grey*. William Morrow (New York, 1986)

Marsh, Carole, *Bill S: Shakespeare for Kids*. Gallopade Publishing Group (Bath, 1983)

Miles, B., *Favorite Tales from Shakespeare*. Macmillan (New York, 1977)

Minard, Rosemary, *Long Meg*. Pantheon Books (New York, 1982)

Turner, Dorothy, *Queen Elizabeth I*. Watts, Franklin (New York, 1987)

Turner, Dorothy, *William Shakespeare*. Watts, Franklin (NY, 1985)

White-Thompson, Stephen, *Elizabeth I and Tudor England*. Watts, Franklin (New York, 1985)

Zamoyska, Betka, *Queen Elizabeth I*. McGraw-Hill (New York, 1981)

INDEX

Masters and Fellows, Corpus Christi College